It was hot. We had been out for three days and nights.

My LRP team of five men and myself hadn't seen anything except regular jungle activity and heard jungle noises.

We had observed a large tree across a field and I decided to make that tree our overnight defensive position. We had no more set up our claymore mines when there came a large group of people heading straight toward our position.

It was dark, but you could see their silhouettes clearly. They came within 10 feet of our claymores.

I didn't want to kill anybody, but they just kept coming.

To! Ted Show

From A Bragg

In His Service

Published by Thomas A. Bragg, Sr.

ISBN-10: 1512349186
ISBN-13: 978-1512349184

Special thanks to my wife, Marji Bragg, for all her help and support.

I would like to dedicate this book to my daughter, Tammy Bragg Lovins, her husband, Ricky Lovins, and my grandson, Thomas Bryce Lovins.

NANKIPOOH RANGER

Thomas A. Bragg, Sr.

War brings out the worst in a man. God brings out the best in us all!

It is so very clear to me, the difference between good and evil. When new replacements arrived on the firebase, they would be regular young Americans, clean with clean clothes and clear eyes. After a few missions, they would become combat-hardened. Most would want to kill Charlie, his wife, his children, his dog, his water buffalo and then burn his hooch and in a firefight, become a mad animal. The pure devil would come out in most, but even in combat those who served God were better soldiers. Back home, they were better husbands, fathers and citizens. These true believers are what makes America great.

When the majority of America was Christian, you could leave your doors unlocked and everybody worked. The time is coming when you will see Christians being persecuted here in our country like they are being killed in the Middle East today.

Thomas A. Bragg, Sr.

Table of Contents

Introduction

Ranger Buddies
A True Story - By Max W. Haney

For years it has been my intention to document one of the most memorable and near tragic experiences of my life. And since it has been fifty two years since the experience and I have no access to the original records, I will acknowledge certain memory limitations and in places use approximations.

It is an accepted fact that the Anny Ranger school is one of the most, if not the toughest training course in the U. S. Army; both physically and mentally. It is designed to train and prove selected individual young combat-leaders in special military skills, under stressful combat conditions; in order to gain insight into himself and his fellow comrades.

The following incident took place in the mountains of north Georgia near the city of Dahlonega during the mountain-phase of the ranger school on a cold February morning in Ranger Class #5 of the year 1960. Ranger Class #5 began January 7th and ran through March 9th, 1960. It consisted of the following military personnel: Approximately 150 West Point 2nd Lieutenants, from the graduating class of 1959

1 regular Army Captain

12 regular Anny enlisted men

2 Marine Corps Sergeants

1 Air Force Sergeant

12 Vietnamese and Thailand Lieutenants

1 Australian Officer, Commander Clark; Commandant of the Australian Army.

Of the approximate 180 students only 128 completed the course. Some dropped out for physical reasons, some just quit; some were recycled to another class. Three West Point Officers drowned at Eglin A. F. B. Florida just off the coast of Santa Rosa island during amphibious operations, when an unexpected wind-squall hit and rolled over several of the sixteen-man rafts and broke off two of the unloading-ramps on the LCU's (Landing Craft Utility). Only nine of the original fifteen enlisted men graduated with the class including myself and Ranger Thomas A. Bragg. Upon graduation we both received an on-the-spot promotion.

Tom was from a small town not far from Fort Benning with the strangest name in history, "Nankipooh"; just outside of Columbus. Tom later introduced me to some of the people of Nankipoo; one a self-proclaimed witch named Ethel Lett. It was said that she sometimes worked black magic on her dissenting neighbors using dolls and needles.

She seemed to like Tom very much though; he enjoyed listening to her and I could see that she knew that. We sat, talked, cut and ate cane, spitting the residual husk fibers into a coal bucket near the wood stove in the middle of the one-room shack. Together we talked some about her gift of witchcraft; I tried to make a good impression on her for obvious reasons.

Tom's gift in life was communicating, he always stood out in a crowd; not because of his six foot four frame and extraordinary strength but because he could become an entertainer at a moments notice with his acculturated southern wit and ability to involve others around him into his humorous perspective of life. He could see humor in almost any taxing situation and could skillfully convey that humor, thus easing the tension of stressful and frustrating circumstances by somehow turning it into entertainment.

Tom had an extraordinary ability to read a map (Geological

Survey), or contour maps, used daily by the military. It is a truism that any military leader and especially an infantry commander, no matter what his leadership background is, will lose the respect of his men and his superiors if he cannot read a map and navigate. Tom by far exceeded his peers in this area and could always gain their respect because of it. Tom and I completed the night "land-navigation course" in record-time. It was announced at the morning formation that rangers Bragg and Haney had broken the old "time-record" for the course. Tom jokingly asked if they taught navigation at West Point. The instructors spent most of the day policing up lost 2nd lieutenants scattered all the way from main post to Cassetta, Ga.

Another attribute of his character was that he would never give up at any time, failure was not in his repertoire. We went to life-guard school together at Fort Benning, Georgia. I was not aware that he was a non-swimmer; he could not swim at all. He was told by the primary instructor to return to his unit; he refused. A heated discussion followed; he asked to be allowed to just observe and learn what he could. The instructor agreed to allow it, only with written-permission from his CO, which he obtained. Tom watched and practiced at the other end of the pool alone for two days. He impressed the instructors so much that he was eventually allowed to join the rest of the class. He graduated along with the class as a "certified-Life-Guard" at Fort Benning. This man went from a non swimmer to a life-guard in only two days.

I later asked Tom how was it that you were 21 years old and could not swim; he said that in south Georgia where he grew up cotton-mouths were often spotted in the ponds and water-bodies and even though there were plenty alligators around to keep the population down he just did not like to be around those dang snakes. I said what about the gators? He replied, "sharp teeth sugar."

The Cliff

For safety and control purposes ranger students are teamed up in groups of two called buddy teams. These teams are to train together and stay together throughout the whole nine week school of instruction. Ranger Thomas A. Bragg and I were assigned together as one of these teams. The following short-story is a prime example of why the buddy-teams were formed.

Tom and I have discussed for years this event which only lasted about ten to fifteen seconds at the most, and although we have not always agreed on some of the surrounding details and sequence of the experience, the facts of the incident as I remember them are as follows.

It was a very cold morning in late February in 1960 in the mountains of north Georgia near the town of Dahlonega in an isolated mountain-range, (where the movie "Deliverance" was made a few years later). It was an ideal place to learn "mountain-climbing techniques." We were bivouacked on the mountain in two-man pup tents. After breakfast we stood around shivering for a while drinking coffee and trying to warm our hands on the canteen-cups. We moved by foot to the training-site for a brief orientation on mountain- climbing-techniques and safety-measures. We were then broken down into groups with Tom and I among the first belay groups on the training site. We would later switch off with the other groups to complete our climbing assignments. As a belay team our job was to establish a belay position to assist the climber if necessary, and to secure him if he should fall during his ascent up the cliff.

Our first task was to tie the fixed-end of a 120 foot climbing-rope to a tree or some other stable object, we chose a strong pine tree, tied on and threw the running-end of the rope over the rim of the cliff to a ledge approximately 100 feet below where the climbers would start their ascent. No one was allowed to begin their climb until the belay team was in place and sounded off with a hardy "on belay."

We were required to secure ourselves with a safety-rope fastened around our waist and tied to a nearby tree or other fixed object. We were in the process of doing this when I noticed that the belay-team on our immediate left was having trouble with their belay-line tangling in a small pine tree just below the cliff's rim. I made an impulsive decision to help. I knew both rangers in the belay-team, Ranger Dobbs and Ranger Rushing.

My good intentions turned out to be a bad mistake. Between our two belay positions was a sheet-of-ice formed by melted-snow. The ice was about one inch thick and approximately 10 feet across with frozen dead grass and weeds protruding through the ice. I knew that I should not walk across that ice which sloped down and spilled over the cliff's rim; but being of analytical mind I decided that the grass and weeds protruding through the ice would allow for a good foothold; (I was wrong). I took about three steps. The last thing I remember hearing was a partial statement from Tom, "quote": "Better let me hold on too!" then the crackling and crunching began to saturate my senses - I could feel the grass and weeds grinding under my boots.

What happened after that is a blur in my memory except for three visual snapshots which will be engraved in my mind forever. First, the helpless, shocked, look on Ranger Dobbs and Ranger Rushings faces when the crackling and crunching began. Secondly a snapshot of the clear empty blue sky as I lay on my back suspended in time sliding toward the rim of the cliff. The last snapshot was that of Tom with his nose in my face in a military manner chewing my ass out; using certain coded expletives unfit for any mother's son to hear, but frequently used and accepted as standard military jargon . I had often in the past rebuked him for his selection of obscene words; this time I did not. In fact the fluid stream of profanity was somewhat comforting, I felt strangely euphoric, I was still alive. And somehow I was aware that this butt-chewing in process was coming from a genuine ranger-buddy; someone who for some unknown reason to me had just risked his life for mine.

Although I was very happy to be alive I began to feel very foolish; It was hard to shake it. It followed me around like a shadow for days. Sometime later my mind finally decoded Tom's message in snapshot three, it read; "Stupid is as stupid does." The chain of happenings between the last two snapshots have been issues of discussion with Tom and I over the years, although they were only minor concerns; like can he hold on to my safety rope? Will he go over the rim with me? Is it even possible to hold on: will he intentionally let go to save himself? etc., etc.!

It is important to note certain impeding facts at this point;

1. A nylon climbing rope is only 7/16 of an inch in diameter, very slippery and hard to hold on to.

2. Tom had grabbed and held on to my safety rope using only one hand.

3. He was holding on to the belay line with his other hand, same diameter nylon.

4. I was hanging over the rim when he stopped me.

5. I had nothing to hold on to at first except my own safety rope which Tom was holding too.

6. The temperature was below freezing and we were very cold.

7. With the leather gloves we had on it was very difficult to hold onto the ropes.

8. These nylon climbing ropes are made to freely slide through a snap-link or carabiner with ease. With a lot of screaming discussion,

and Tom with his heels dug in we were somehow able to get my body back over the rim of the diffusing both the belay-line and my safety-line. Tom's hold on my safety rope caused my body to be pulled over the ice to my right during my descent such that I was able somehow to grab the belay-line. I guess I can always say, "I was the first ranger over the rim that day." However, if one of the cadri instructors had been present at the time, Tom would probably have received an unsatisfactory spot-report for not yelling; "On Belay."

There are a lot of "what ifs," that could be mentioned here such as:

1. What if Tom had not been watching when I started to cross the ice?

2. What if he had not taken the precaution of grabbing the loose end of my safety rope when I started to cross the ice?

3. What if Tom had not been in position to grab hold of the belay line fixed to the tree? What if I had been teamed with some ranger other than Tom? Would he have been able, or even willing to do what Tom did? Tom was a very strong person. I suppose that the "what ifs" could go on and on but one thing is for certain and it too is an "If." "If" I owe my life to any one person on earth, it is Ranger Thomas A. Bragg. He was a skillful leader with an uncanny ability to be in the right place at the right time and do the right thing.

That evening after training I reported to the T.A.C officer's tent; explained the incident to the T.A.C. officer and T.A.C. NCO. The response I received from them was two blank faces of awe and wonder. They thanked me for reporting the incident. I left.

I never heard another word about it, either from the T.A.C. officers or any of the school cadri - Tom didn't either. We often wondered if the event was ever noted for the record or just buried under the tragic deaths of the three West Point officers at Santa Rosa Island. Anyway, it is not logical to believe that anyone could hold on to a small nylon climbing rope with a 170 pound screaming ranger on the end of it - with only one hand. On my 60th birthday my family gave me a surprise party, Tom was there. We told the story to my family and friends, some clapped with approval, others had that same blank stare of awe that I witnessed in the T.A.C. officers tent.

This unselfish act of comradery seems to have gone on unheralded and appreciated only by me. My life was given back to me because of a buddy's quick thinking; and the fact that he was in the right-place at the right-time doing the right-thing. I wondered if my 29 children, grandchildren and great-grandchildren could even understand the "gravity" of this event: for ten or fifteen seconds, my ranger buddy had in his hands the very posterity of their very existence.

For this I would like to say Thank You, to Ranger Thomas A. Bragg.

Lived and prepared by Ranger Max W. Haney

CHAPTER 1 -- THE NANKIPOOH NORMAL

Sitting around now at home by my fireplace, looking outside at a small pond, pecan trees, a grape vine and a nice swimming pool in a beautiful subdivision, I think about how it is a far cry from my early days in 1940's Nankipooh, Georgia, when I was just the son of Inez Pittman and Thomas Howard Bragg.

My father was a large man, standing six-foot-three at 240 pounds. He worked for Central of Georgia Railroad as a flagman. That was one of those jobs that went right on working, even during the depression. ln 1942, my father bought 320 acres, at $3 an acre, in Harris County, Georgia, about 18 miles out Whitesville Road, north of Columbus. He went three miles off Whitesville Road down a two-rut trail to build a three-room house with a back porch.

Dad was quite a builder. He used pine trees on rocks for the foundation and slabs left over from the sawmill for outside walls. He did a wonderful job, even though most everything he used was left over or given to him. The house had a window and a door in front and back. Both had a board that locked from the inside. We had what was called a lock string that hung through a hole outside, so you could pull a board up inside to unlock the door.

We had a wood stove and a well right next to the back porch where you could stand on the porch and draw water. Dad and another man dug this forty feet well in three days. We had a log with a handle and as the log turned the rope rolled around it and we could raise the bucket up and down to draw water right up to the porch. There was a small weight on one side of the bucket so it would sink sideways in the water. Our bathroom was a one-seat outhouse about 75 feet behind the home.

Mother cooked with a wood stove. Since we lived in the middle of the woods, we had more to burn than anybody else. This house sat so far back among the trees our mailbox sat three miles at the end of our driveway on Whitesville Road. We lived there with my half-brother Don, myself, my brother Jimmy, who is four years younger than me, and my sister Blair, who is two years younger than Jimmy.

Our closest neighbors were Earl and Dora Simms, who lived five miles down the road. They had a farm with cows, hogs, chickens, a barn and a smokehouse. You name it, they had it, except for a well. They had a spring that came out from under a big rock. It was cool, clear water. They kept butter and milk down in the spring and kept hams and other meats hanging in the smokehouse. That spring of water was about 100 feet downhill west of their house. Out back was a large clear area going about 150 yards with outbuildings on both sides, along with everything from chicken houses to hog pens.

I loved to go over there. They had mules and horses, as well as a barn east the house down a hill. I don't know how much land they had, but I do know that they had a large field down in the bottom where they grew corn and other things. This field had a creek running down one side and under the road. There was mostly rock in and around the creek. During summer, Earl and Dora would have 10 to 15 teenagers come to live with them from "up north." I was only five or six years old, but I remember Earl hitting them with switches to make them work. He said after being up north they weren't worth anything. "They won't work. They just wait for someone to bring it to them," he'd say. My experience was much better. Eating at Earl and Dora's was the very best. We feasted on fresh vegetables and salty ham with all the milk and butter -- real butter -- you wanted.

One night Earl came to our house around 11 p.m. and said that his oldest son, Hyde, was very sick. Earl wanted daddy to take him to Columbus in our car, being afraid their old truck wouldn't make it that far. I believe Hyde died a few days later from complications of some kind. The Simms family and mine were good friends. We visited regularly until we moved.

Living far into the woods was scary, especially when the sun started setting and darkness arrived. We had candles, but they didn't give much light. One morning about 9 o'clock, some Army trucks pulled in our yard. "What in the world!" my mother said. "Nobody ever comes up our driveway, especially four or five Army vehicles." They began unloading prisoners of war from Ft. Benning. These were Italian prisoners sent to work on the roads. This is when we learned that our driveway used to be the old road to Mulberry Grove, Georgia. They continued to come around for about a month. I recall they called my mother Bambino, or baby.

Not far from our house was an old two story plantation house that had fallen down. Most of it was overgrown with bushes. There was a very tall black woman who lived there. I remember that she was very black and very stately, so tall and upright. We never knew who all lived there, but a young teenaged girl stayed there some of the time. There was never a car or horse or wagon, no form of transportation there. We never knew how they lived. Earl told us that years ago the white folks living there just up and moved and those who were left there did the best they could.

One day mother told me to go get the mail and as I walked past this big old house this tall lady asked me where I was going and said that I was so young. I replied that I was going to the mailbox. She said that it was too far for me to go by myself and told this teenaged girl to go with me. I had never heard the girl say a word and she didn't say anything that day until we got about halfway to the main road and suddenly an airplane flew over us.

This girl ran down a washout and hid under a bush and I ran after her. She was afraid the "bird" would eat her. This is the truth. This family didn't have a mailbox or any sign of communication with the outside world. Someone told me that they ate possum and poke salad, which is simply wild greens.

You can imagine all the problems living that far out back in those days. The roads were mostly red clay and rocks. It was all but impossible to travel on when it rained. I remember one morning mother was ready to go to town after it had rained. There was a small hill that was completely covered in red clay and it could put you in the ditch if you didn't drive carefully. We came around the bend in the road so that we could see the hill. Two cars and a truck were already sideways. Mother never slowed down at all. In fact, she sped up. Some men who were pushing the stuck vehicles tried to get out of her way the best they could. She went between and around them and their cars and over the hill.

Daddy worked on the Cedartown run, on what is called "the road" in railroad terminology. He was gone two nights and home one night. Those nights out in the woods by ourselves were rough and scary. Bridges would wash out or float when it rained heavily. The wooden bridges had cables on each side anchored to trees, so the bridges would rise with the water, but when the water went down, the bridges would never go back in place. We would be isolated anywhere from three days to a week until county workers would put the bridges as they were. One bridge floated like this on the way back to Columbus over the Standing Boy Creek and two more like that when going north.

It wasn't much better for those without a car. Most people had horses or mules that pulled wagons and they would drive the wagon down in the water mostly on the downstream side of the bridge and up the bank on the far side. You would see people riding and walking on Friday and Saturday for supplies. They would only go to the first store they came to which was on Hamilton Road. They would only buy what they had to have to survive, such as flour, sugar and salt. Late those same nights, you would see them riding their wagon or walking beside it, trying to get home.

We would try to figure out where all these people lived. They were like us, living way back off the main road. I guess they didn't want others to see how hard they had it. Most had a two- or three-room house with no electricity or plumbing, perhaps with a mule, chickens, hogs, a small garden, and of course a dog or several. Coon hunting was a big thing. Many of these people ate coon or possum, poke salad and turnip greens on a regular basis.

One memorable day in 1945, we were returning from town after picking daddy up from work and buying a week's supply of groceries. Daddy offered a ride to a young black man, maybe 25 years old, walking down the road. He had nothing with him -- no bag and not even a hat. He was wearing pants, shirt and some old brogan shoes that laced up and around the ankle.

The man, whose name we learned was Gage, was clean and very nice and polite, but it made for a crowded ride with daddy, mother, Don, Jimmy, Blair, myself and this young man in a 1941 Ford two-door car. And, no, I didn't sit in anybody's lap. I laid in the back window where the sun was shining. I just fit there as a six year old. The driver couldn't see through the rear view mirror, but who cared? We had the windows down and dust was flying in and behind the car.

We were going home on this red clay road at about 35 or 45 mph. when we saw black and white smoke over the tree tops. We saw a forest fire burning everything in it's path as we crossed the bridge over Standing Boy Creek.

Flames reached the tops of 60-foot-high pine trees. The bad thing about this fire was the wind blowing north toward our house, with the road between our house and the blaze. Daddy said our only hope to save our home was to stop the fire from jumping the road. He stopped the car, then ran across the road and jumped a six-foot ditch. He broke the top off a young pine tree and used it to put the fire out. These woods were difficult to walk through, let alone fight fire in, but it had to be stopped, not only to save our house, but others in danger.

Don didn't have much luck crossing the ditch. Then I noticed this young black man had run up the road to a break in the fire that jumped the road. He lept over the ditch and grabbed a pine top like dad did. With each swat of that tree top they would put out five to seven feet of fire. Don finally crossed the ditch mopping up what was left of the fire after dad did his thing.

Thomas Bragg was a mountain of a man. His fit body was huge with large round muscles. Dad put the fire out up to the break where Gage was. Gage's shirt caught on fire, but he tore it off and never stopped. While dad's body was large and thick, Gage had fine, defined muscles. He was almost as tall as dad, but not as heavy.

Seeing these large men's teamwork fighting this fire was a sight to behold among the heat and cinder flying everywhere. Their clothes and hair and skin were burned, but they kept attacking along the line of fire. The powerful duo beat back a wall of flame and, at times, disappeared into the smoke and blaze. Their muscular frames would reappear with sweat and blood running down them.

My mother played protector. "Get back, come here. Y'all are crazy," she yelled while grabbing Blair and Jimmy and retreating down the road. Don was far down the fire line by then and he was doing a good job quelling small flames that crept up. It was easier to put out the fire when the wind stopped blowing and the fire just quit moving. Mother said it was because she was praying to God. Daddy was thankful, because the fire wasn't long before getting out of hand.

"I wish I had not accepted the ride," Gage said with a laugh. We all fell down for a good chuckle, relieved that the fire was out. This was the first time I saw men look at each other with such respect and friendship, born of teamwork and accomplishment. This is the same kind of fellowship I would later see in Vietnam while serving in the 101st Airborne and the U. S. Army Ranger C and G Companies.

After our bout with danger, three men in a pickup truck arrived saying they were there to put out the fire. We loaded up with daddy, Gage, and Don in the front seat and mother, myself, Jimmy and Blair, the baby, in the back. We insisted Gage come home with us, where mother started cooking her soup -- which meant put everything in a big pot and cook. Daddy, Gage and Don were on the back porch naked, pouring water from the well over each other. This seemed so barbaric to mother. "You cook and we'll wash," daddy said.

Not that it did much good. They still looked bad, with cuts, burns and most all hair singed off their heads and bodies. Daddy gave Gage some clothes that were too small for him and some new brogan shoes with a steel toe, which is what they wore at the railroad.

Daddy and Gage talked about several things while we sat around after the meal, such as work, President Roosevelt and Civilian Conservation Corps (CCC) camps. Gage said he worked at a CCC camp on Pine Mountain for three years and he would be glad when the war was over. He said goodbye after resting, but wouldn't take a ride to wherever he was going. He just walked down the road and we never saw him again. Daddy said for years that God must have sent Gage that day or the whole county would have burned up. Mother insisted it was her prayers that stopped that fire. Either way, thanks to God, daddy and Gage.

We moved to Nankipooh soon after that, where Daddy built a log house. We mixed mud and water and packed it between the logs. It had two rooms, plus a kitchen-like room This house was fine to us because that's all we knew. We had hogs and chickens and plenty of work in the garden.

There weren't many around us who could say their life was easy. Lots of folks were employed at cotton mills, where work was demanding and it was hard to stay ahead. People would borrow money to buy from the company commissary and by the time pay-day come around they owed most of their income to the commissary. Then they would have to buy everything else in the commissary because they owed their soul to the store.

My momma swore if any of her kids worked in a cotton mill, she'd kill them. She went to work in a cotton mill at 12 years old and stayed until she started having children. Momma had to quit school around fifth grade, though she could spell anything, even if she was country. She never wanted anything else to do with the cotton mill.

Some workers also lived in the cotton mills' company housing. It was rough for area people and those who moved to Columbus from South Georgia and South Alabama to work at cotton mills. If you asked people working in those Columbus mills, they would say, "I'm just from down home," and you would know they were from Dothan or Enterprise, Alabama because everybody was from "down home."

No doubt times were hard. It didn't help when the boll weevil rolled in. That hungry pest ate away at cotton buds and ruined the crop. There was even a song written about the boll weevil just look-ing for a home. Well, it actually worked out. As many times in life, the good Lord had a better thing coming, because after the boll wee-vil destroyed cotton plants, people started planting soybeans and other crops. Turns out they did so well with the new row crops that they made a boll weevil statue somewhere in South Alabama. You could ride through town and see a monument for the boll weevil, which had changed the course of farming.

I started school when I turned six. My 10-year-old half brother, Donald Brown, was already enrolled at Mt. Hill school. The school was 20 miles out Whitesville Road from Earl and Dora's house. Don and I had to catch the school bus at Earl and Dora's house to get there. If we walked down our driveway and turned right on Whitesville Road it would be between five and six miles, but if we cut out west through the woods it would was about one or two miles.

There was no trail and no road for the short route, but we had two creeks to cross with many rocks in them. There were fallen trees, briars, bushes and wait-a-minute vines. It was a small adventure for young boys like us. And we never went the same way twice. It was a dangerous way to get to the bus stop, but we made it on time most days. If we missed the bus, we just played around on our way back home, crossing the two creeks and walking a mile or so through dense woods, with plenty of opportunity to check things out. Many times I fell in one or both creeks. We would see all kinds of animals like bobcats, bears and even black panthers.

One of my first memories from the early days of school involved needing to go to the bathroom during recess. If it was "Number 1", we would go outside behind a tree. This, however, was much more serious. I asked other kids where the bathroom was, but this was grade school and they sent me the wrong way. The could only laugh as they watched me struggle to hold my bowels. It was too late.

When we returned to class, the teacher said, "someone" has stepped in "something." She checked our feet. My left foot was fine. Then she asked to see my other foot. "It" had run down my leg to my right foot. Before I knew it the teacher pulled my desk with me in it out into the hall. The smell was so bad that when the janitor opened the door at the end of the long hall, he stepped back outside. Nobody would get near me at the bus stop, either. All the kids opened windows and put their heads outside when I got on the bus. What a day of shame for me. I guess things like this happen more than we would like to think about back in those days.

You might say things didn't get much better from there. I was in first grade for three years and second grade for two years because I couldn't read. They would move me up eventually. By the time I reached fifth grade, I was a confirmed idiot. I had report cards with nothing but F's. Not an A, B, C or D. Just plain F's. But they moved me right along until the eighth grade, when I left at age 16. I tried to go back when I was 17, but I didn't last long. They told me I couldn't go to ninth grade because I didn't pass eighth grade. I didn't see why not. They had moved me all the way from first grade regardless of what I knew.

I couldn't read. I couldn't write. I didn't know what was wrong. Luck did have it that I was good as some things in school. Matter of fact, I could knock a home run most anytime I wanted to being 15 years old in the seventh grade. Sometimes people from the city with whom we played ball would see us getting out of the trucks and just decide they'd put their little kids back in the car, go home and forfeit the game.

I also got to befriend several characters growing up in Nankipooh.

There was a man named Edgar, wasn't lined up just right. He hardly associated with anyone. The city bus from Columbus ran to Hog Cash Grocery and back. Edgar rode the bus daily to work at a cotton mill, but on Saturdays he went to the movie matinee. He loved seeing cowboy movies. Us kids would play back there between our house and the main part of Nankipooh, which was around Hog Cash Grocery, the only store in town. You'd see Edgar running through the woods from over there at Hog Cash Grocery, sprinting from tree to rock, occasionally rolling on the ground, shooting his finger like he was a cowboy. He was fun to watch. I don't know what ever happened to ol' Edgar

There was another fella who'd been in the second World War. Merkel Grimes was a little fellow with a disability from the war. He dug wells for people around Nankipooh and took any odd jobs he could get. Merkel would sometimes have me help him pull buckets of dirt up while he was down in the wells digging. He always had something funny to say and like to spout riddles and rhymes, like, "Shoo fly, shoo. Apple pandowdy. Make your eyes light up, your stomach say howdy."

Merkel had set up a small camp at the end of a pond among the brush of woods. Merkel would fish and make do with that little pension he had. The land owners never came around, so they didn't know about him. It was like going to Adventure Island when visiting Merkel's place. He had ropes tied up and trot lines out. He used his tiny check to buy what he had to have. I thought it was a neat place, with a camper back into the brush and a dock built on the pond. The property owner who finally discovered what was going on didn't see it that way and ran Merkel off.

Merkel then moved to a hill, where he bought his own lot and an old school bus. In true Merkel fashion, he dug the school bus into the ground for a makeshift home. Kids liked to stop by and see the place. It had a half-underground room that let sunlight in to stay warm in the winter, but he could go farther down the hole in the bus to stay cool in summer. He would tell us kids that we had garments and ancestors and we had better go and clean up.

But Merkel also worked a lot. He would dig deep wells here and there, getting anyone he could to help him. He dug wells, getting cold and freezing down there. It's cold in a well, now. If you do a well you get down in the bottom and put the dirt in the bucket. When they pull the bucket up, the mud and the water splashes down on top of you. No where to go but on you at the bottom. Sometimes, the reason I know, is Merkel got me to go down in the well and dig some while he pulled up the bucket. I was only 12 or 13 years old at that time, but I couldn't pass at school and nobody could figure out what was wrong with me.

I never thought Merkel would live long, considering his lifestyle. Turns out he only recently died -- at 99 years old. He outlived everyone there in Nankipooh during that time. That's something for a little bitty man with a war disability, something wrong with him, who lived underground and with mosquitos around that pond.

And let me tell you about John Henry Dawson -- a boy who was worse off than I was, bless his heart. John Henry was big, healthy and strong, but couldn't pass in school. He lived farther back in the woods than I did. I don't think John Henry ever had a pair of shoes in his life. His toes were swollen all the time from where he stumped them on rocks and roots.

One memory that sticks out about John Henry was from about third or fourth grade when we had a substitute teacher. Most of our teachers in Nankipooh were pretty old and rough. They were past their prime, but they sort of knew how to handle us younguns. This substitute teacher must not have been more than 23 years old.

John Henry and I were sitting back of the room when a little girl stepped on John Henry's big toe, which was already sore from banging it on other things. That man-child let out a huge yelp, collapsed to the floor, put that big toe in his mouth and started sucking on the sore. After the initial shock, the young teacher scolded him to get that nasty toe out of his mouth. John Henry wouldn't quit sucking on that toe and kept going for a while. Now don't get me wrong. John Henry was a good guy, but he was often involved in some crazy times.

Momma once had me cut down an oak tree in our yard with a crosscut saw and, after it laid there for a year, we chopped it into firewood for the stove. I took an iron pipe and drove it down into the middle of the stump. Then I drilled a hole in the middle of a 2'x8' board and put it over that iron stake on top of the stump. My brothers and sisters would get on both ends of the board and ride it as I pushed them around. We called it the Flying Jenny.

We ended up placing a good bit of heavy-duty grease on the stump after neighbors starting coming over wanting to ride and suggested we do that so it would really slide around fast. It got so popular we had adults showing up to ride the Flying Jenny.

One day, however, big John Henry showed up wanting to ride. No matter how many people we put on the other side of the board, he was too heavy to balance with anybody. We finally told him all he could do was push it.

"I'll tell you what I'll do then. Y'all just hang on," John Henry said.

He was pretty mad by this point, so I got on one side and my two brothers on the other. We were hanging on near a little ditch we built around that stump for running around the Flying Jenny. John Henry started pushing us so fast, the centrifugal force almost threw us off the board. I was holding on with my feet sticking out into the air as John Henry furiously spun us around. He was determined to to get back at us for him being unable to ride (like it was our fault).

His plan went awry when he tripped. No more than he'd fallen that the board came back around and hit him in the back of the head. John Henry tried again to get up again and got smacked by the board once more. Then again and again. He was bellowing like a bull by this point. We ran while he was stuck on the ground, and buddy, every one of us kids hid under the house, in ditches or in trees because John Henry got up with knots all over his head. That was one mad human. John Henry wouldn't try to ride the Flying Jenny any more after that. He actually told everybody we tried to kill him.

I saw him years later while I was home on leave from the Army. There was a car coming down the dirt road on the big hill in front of our house. There were heads of youngins sticking out every window as it coasted, then shut off. I headed to the bottom of the hill to help and out stepped John Henry, with his six head of kids and a big, fat wife. We caught up a bit as we watched the car's radiator boil over. John Henry said he was a logging man. He looked like a big, hairy gorilla, but it was nice to see him one more time years later.

There's so much I could say about living in Nankipooh. I know after all these years you become part of your environment.

Life in the Bragg household, at times, probably seems a bit unusual to many folks nowadays.

There was a time when momma ordered 100 chicken bitties through the mail. Yep, through the mail. They soon grew into pullets. It wasn't too long after that we found an escaped monkey, from where we didn't know, which was starving to death. We fed him, but he stayed chained in the backyard. The monkey's health returned during our care. He would jump and scratch and act funny. It was great entertainment.

As time passed we started finding dead pullets here and there. Momma stationed my other brother and me around our bomb shelter to discover the killer. (Momma often had me dig bomb shelters because we were afraid the Russians were coming. She believed in keeping me busy with hard labor. I once dug a basement for a house one summer, around 60 x 20 feet.)

We hid behind our well and crept around to spy on the monkey. He was nonchalant for the most part. That was his act until he thought he was alone as a chicken came by scratching and picking. Mr. Monkey grabbed that young hen, put its head under his arm and started putting his finger in the chicken's behind. He tried to have sex with the chicken. Sure did!

And that was just the beginning of the monkeying around.

My brother ran and told momma what the monkey did. She stormed out hollering at that animal with such force her false teeth flew out her mouth. The monkey grabbed her upper plate, bit a hole in it and ran up a tree with his new prize. Momma called for me and I came running to chase down the monkey. He finally dropped momma's teeth while jumping from branch to branch. From then on, she had a raw place in the top of her mouth from the hole in her plate. Momma never liked the monkey after that episode.

He eventually escaped to the woods to feast on blackberries and whatever he could find. But once the weather cooled and it rained for a few days straight, he scurried back to our house for cover.

One of our neighbors down the road, Ms. Rogers, happened to hear a noise outside her home one of these times. She opened the door and that monkey -- by then cold, nasty and unable to control his bodily functions -- climbed Ms. Rogers and hugged her head to get warm. She screamed bloody murder.

Ms. Rogers was a no-nonsense woman and you know she meant business when you saw her walking a country block from her house, though the rain, and started beating on our door. I answered and saw Ms. Rogers there, still wearing the rascal around her head.

"Get yo' monkey off my back!" she demanded in a moment that was difficult for me not to laugh, despite her fury.

The monkey had become sick with pneumonia, so we put him on the porch in a little box, like a baby crib, and wrapped him tightly in a blanket. We gave him milk and medicine, trying to get him well. He couldn't stay in the house. We tried keeping him inside once before, but he turned over everything and messed everywhere.

Momma had been keeping me out of school at this time. She

claimed there wasn't a need for me to go to school anyhow, because I couldn't learn anything. My frequent absence finally drew a visit from the school truant officer. Momma did not like anyone messing with her business. The truant officer interrogated my mother about why I wasn't in school. My momma nearly jumped on her.

"Can't you see all these youngins I got here? I got to have some help with all these children."

The truant officer was unphased and was particularly upset about one "child" she spotted outside.

"You ought to be in jail for having this baby out here on this porch in all this cold," she scolded.

"Well, if you think he's ugly, you ought to have seen his daddy!" momma snapped back. The truant officer left and hasn't come back yet. She didn't bother us about going to school any more.

My life growing up wasn't in any way right, but it was all I knew. So when momma got into telling fortunes and reading coffee grounds in a cup, we just went along with it. Her friends and she would go up country to Meriwether County, past Callaway Gardens before Newnan. There was a lady there called Mayhayley Lancaster, whose life was the subject of the book, "Oracle of the Ages."

Mayhayley was said to have had a "veil" on her face at birth, empowering her to tell fortunes. People came from miles around to hear their fortunes, including my momma, my Aunt Lelett and anybody else they could get to join them.

This fascinating lady would sit in a room inside an old slab house on a dirt road. You would pay to get in and Mayhayley would tell you how much money you had. That's how she charged. If you were rich, she charged a lot. If you didn't have any money, she wouldn't ask much, according to momma.

During my mother's first visit, Mayhayley spoke of momma's baby brother being killed in Luxembourg, Germany in the second

World War. Mayhayley said a person momma loved very much died over across the sea and his initials were R.L. That's what they called him: R.L. Pittman. From then on, my momma took stock in Mayhayley Lancaster.

I remember Mayhayley had a glass eye and long black hair. She'd stand around and peep out the door and us children had to wait outside. She would sit in a chair, go into a trance, wake up and tell you something, then go back and talk like she's asleep. Momma and Aunt Lelett bought spells from her to put on folks. I can tell you myself these spells seemed to work on some people. Mayhayley may be long gone, but I don't try to talk much about her spells and witchcraft. I tried to stay away from that stuff as much as I could.

People would buy spells and Mayhayley would tell them what to do. For example, you'd need to get something belonging to the target person, put it in something else and hide it somewhere they would go. It was supposed to cause the victim harm when passing by.

I don't know if the spell worked or the people just had misfortune, but every time they put a spell on somebody, those people had a bunch of trouble. I'm serious! I don't believe in witchcraft and stuff, but they sure did.

When people came to our house, the first thing momma did was tell their fortune. She also wouldn't let anyone come in the front door and leave out the back, because if you didn't go back out the front door, you supposedly left all your troubles at the place you visited. And if the first person to visit you on New Year's morning is a woman, you have bad luck the whole year. If a man is the first visitor, you have good luck. So they say, anyway.

Poor ol' Ms. Rogers came to our home one New Year's and momma cussed her out because she was bringing bad luck. These tales go all the way back to old folk tales from the North Georgia mountains. People put a lot of stock in things like that back where I grew up. Being someone who couldn't learn in school, that stuff sort of stayed with me.

Though I was still a teenager, I was in my early years of manhood. I worked pulling a cross-cut saw to cut big virgin pine when I was 15 and 16 years old. This was older, rugged pine, not new soft pine. That's as hard as it gets, working from daylight to dark, or from can until can't. Many days I would only make it to the living room floor when I left work and I would lie there until morning. I plugged on day to day, at least until I started passing blood. A doctor came to our house and said I would die if I didn't eat some "real" food.

That sounds like a simple solution. Common sense, even, but our life in Nankipooh was far from normal for many folks.

My mother told me that I had to leave because she couldn't feed me and all my five little brothers and sisters by herself.

My father passed away from leukemia two years earlier when I was about 15 years old. It was a slow death that took a year and was hard to witness. The mountain of a man went from 240 pounds to around 100 pounds when he passed. I would fan him with a pine limb to keep the insects off him. A friend of ours said the saddest thing he had ever seen was the widow and all those kids standing around daddy's grave when he was buried.

I had to leave, but I had no where to go. I was tall and thin as a pole, not able to read or write, but I was not forsaken.

Our family wasn't church-going people, but I found myself at a revival two years earlier on a Wednesday night. I was part of a Boy Scout troop brought into a prayer meeting. I loved being part of the boys, even though they sometimes made fun of me. They told me to go up during the altar call, since they had already done it.

The preacher said that God would never leave us and he would help us wherever we go. I wasn't sure what I was doing, but I felt compelled to step out in the aisle. Everything was so clean and serene. I didn't see anyone and I don't remember speaking with the preacher or leaving the church. There were only beautiful crystal white lights around me. It was like a tunnel of wonderful brightness surrounded me. You don't forget moments like that.

The next day or so I went job hunting downtown, but there was no work for an uneducated 17 year old like me. Fortunately, a higher power was leading me to a higher calling.

CHAPTER 2 -- COUNTRY BOY READY TO SERVE HIS COUNTRY

There was nowhere to go when I took my first steps of forced independence. I was 17 and didn't know what to do as I left home. The journey began when I packed a lunch and went walking to Columbus. Each business rejected me when I asked for a job. My appearance couldn't have helped. I had a shaved head, teeth covered in cavities and was in pretty bad shape. I was sad, but I really didn't know how sad I was until I look back on it now.

Fortunately, the local Army recruiter was glad to see a warm body step through his door in the Broadway area of Columbus. He said he would try to get me in and handed me a test. After telling him I could read "a little," the friendly recruiting sergeant advised me just to mark "C" if I didn't know an answer, because that letter was the most-likely to be the answer. Well, I marked "C" a lot. I got 28 questions correct -- out of 100.

I wasn't smart but I was lucky, apparently. He told me the Army was running a "special" that if a high school graduate made 80 or above on the test, he could send a Category IV like me. A "CAT IV" score was from 16 to 32, meaning you barely had enough sense to walk around by yourself. Fortunately, the persistent recruiter had a real smart graduate leaving the next day and said he could still send me to Atlanta for a physical if I returned by noon the next day with my mother's signed permission to join the Army. He also noticed I was underweight, so he told me to eat all I could that night.

Momma had me back down there by 11 o'clock the next morning. The recruiter took the other future soldier and me to a restaurant and let us order anything we wanted. He put us on the bus and gave me a big bag of bananas with instructions to eat all of them because I was underweight. I liked that kind of welcome. The next day we got to Atlanta and they fed us yet again as soon as we got off the bus that night. And to make sure we packed on every pound we could before our physical, they fed us another big meal and gave us a physical. We later boarded a bus bound for Ft. Jackson, South Carolina -- after another meal.

I felt like I was one of the boys once I arrived, except my head was already shaved because that's what my momma did. The only difference after they shaved the other recruits is that they were white-headed, without sunburn like me. At least I looked better bald than they did.

They gave us a bunch of tests at Ft. Jackson, which again meant I was marking a lot of C's on the answer sheet. After two or three tests, in which I was the first to complete each one, the proctor asked if I had any college. I thought I must be doing really good. Then he sent me down the hall to report to the officer in charge.

The officer asked what was wrong with me since I was marking so many C's. I said I couldn't read too well and told him about the recruiter's strategy for questions I didn't know how to answer. The officer wondered if I couldn't or just had problems seeing, so he had me read an eye chart, then again backwards as well as spell out letters written on a diploma hanging in the room. Then he had his answer.

"You have the worst case of dyslexia I've ever seen," he said bluntly.

"No, I've never had dyslexia, but I've had chicken pox, measles, mumps and such," I replied.

"You can't possibly read or write. You can't stay in the Army. How did you get this far?"

I felt my future slipping away. I started crying, begging for a chance. "What's wrong with you? Stop that crying right now," he barked.

I explained my father had died two years earlier and my mother couldn't feed me anymore with so many hungry mouths at home. I recounted walking the road with just a sack lunch as each place turned me down for a job -- until I met the Army recruiter.

"If you let me stay in the Army, I'll make the best soldier you ever saw."

The officer stared downward at the desk. I felt words pass through my mind.

He will never leave you or forsake you. Never.

I think that may have been the first time I realized God Almighty stepped in to help me, because that officer didn't have to let me in the Army. He told me to quit crying and go to the waiting room. When the others came out, I was to fall in with them. That man broke the rules because of compassion in his heart, when he could have sent me back to Columbus. He had to write my name on those test and fill them out to a certain point. When scores were released at basic training, I had a General Testing score of 98. That's not really good, because it's out of 160, but it was better than some recruits. I give God credit for seeing me into the Army when I wasn't really qualified. The officer said I'd be in the infantry, so there would always be others around. Maybe some of them would read for me.

Basic training was wonderful. How could I not like it? They fed you three meals each day and all the chocolate milk you could drink. You got two pairs of boots and all kinds of clothing. We got money to spend at the PX on soap, a toothbrush, razor blades and even things to display in our locker. We never used them, just looked at them. I didn't understand why, so I asked a sergeant who took time to explain it.

"There's a right way and a wrong way and the Army way. Don't ask any more stupid questions."

Not everyone was thrilled with me, however. The other fellas said I was a stupid hillbilly or that I was slow and country. They said I fell off of the turnip truck and that I was plumb dumb. Sergeants and everybody else made me do push-ups and sit-ups all the time. I ended up doing more push-ups and sit-ups than anyone in the company. I pulled Kitchen Patrol more than anyone, but I liked that even if they said I was crazy for enjoying KP. Some boys were really hard on me. They made fun of me and pulled tricks. I really didn't mind too much, because I was one of these boys.

One trick happened following a 20-mile march to the firing range. We had a shelter half and we butted up with another fella's shelter half to make a tent. Everybody had three poles and you had two little ropes and tent pegs. There was an uneven number of people in my platoon, so of course I ended up with a half-tent. I made shelter by placing my tent on the side of a hill. The wind was blowing on that side, but I had enough sense to fix my tent like that under a tree. I think it wound up the best one out there.

That night of camping at the firing range was also the first time I'd seen anyone shot. One boy in the next tent over shot himself in the foot with an M-1 rifle. He rolled on the ground, screaming in terrible pain with his foot messed up. I tried to help, but I didn't know what to do. Others were telling him medics were coming. Everybody later said he shot himself on purpose to get out of basic training.

Next day on the firing range, I was in the first shooting group to qualify. When you shot a target, they would lower it, see where you hit, mark it with discs and raise it up. If you missed the whole target, they'd waive a red flag called Maggie's Drawers. Everybody would laugh if you missed that badly. I qualified expert with the rifle, thanks to learning how to squeeze the trigger from all my squirrel hunting with those boys in Nankipooh.

After qualifying ended, I was surprised to receive a task from our field first sergeant.

"Where's Country?" he called. That was my nickname. He sent word for me to report to him instead of going down to pull target.

"Country, you take this message up to the next firing range to Sgt. Baker," he said. "And you run the whole way and don't you stop, for this is very important, you got me?"

"Yes sergeant!" I replied before heading off without hestitation.

There wasn't time or need to ask further details. I thought I had a special mission. Perhaps the Russians were coming and I was going to save the world.

I started running with the steel pot on my head and canteen flopping at my side, carrying my entrench tool with my harness and poncho rolled up on my back. I had my rifle at port arms running all the way.

The run was about a quarter mile up a dirt road during a scorching August at Ft. Jackson. I sprinted all the way to the other range and hollered for Sgt. Baker, the field first for that company.

"What you want private?"

"Sgt. Jones sent me here with this message."

He analyzed the paper's contents, wrote something and gave it back to me.

"Private, you get that back down there immediately! You run all the way. Don't you stop."

"Right sergeant!"

Then I knew I had a special mission.

Private Bragg darted back down to give Sgt. Jones the message. He also read it and turned away to write on the paper before ordering me to return to Sgt. Baker immediately.

"And Country, I mean run Georgia cracker!" I did as commanded, but I recalled seeing another NCO chuckling before I departed. I stopped halfway to my destination, unfolded the note and looked at this important communication.

They were playing tic-tac-toe. And my bubble burst.

I thought I was doing something as honest as I can be. The disappointment set in and I just fell over on the roadside, exhausted. I laid out with my weapon, soaking with sweat. That's when I heard someone on the range hollering for a medic. Then two aid trucks, one from both ways, revved toward me. Medics started loosening my clothes and pouring water on me.

"He has heatstroke, get back!" one yelled as they carried me by stretcher to the aid truck. Just before they put me in inside, a captain approached to ask if I was all right.

"Sgt. Jones told me to give this to Sgt. Baker," I said, showing the paper.

An ambulance whisked me to the hospital, but the doctor was already gone for the afternoon when I arrived. They weren't sure what to do, so they stuck me in a room until a doctor could see me. It was glorious.

I took a shower then got in a comfy bed with clean sheets. They brought food on a tray. That night I got out of bed wearing pajamas and a robe to go to the chow hall and eat a bunch of stuff. I had three times the dessert and all the chocolate milk I could drink! I capped the evening playing ping-pong and pool with medical staff and other patients. Next morning, I was up, dressed and back to the chow hall for a big breakfast.

It really was a nice place. I walked around the hospital talking to friendly folks. By the time I got back to my room the doctor had already passed by. The extended stay got cut short when he returned to evaluate me.

"What's wrong with you private?

"Heatstroke."

"Heatstroke! Get your stuff and get on back to your unit. You're missing training."

I soon arrived back at the company, but they were still in the field, camped in the woods. A private staying behind to answer phone calls said I could go out there or stay until they got back. That was an easy decision.

I went down to the barracks. Instead of having 50 men in the latrine, I had 10 toilets all to myself. All of the sinks, too. I ultimately stayed in the Army 24 years, but I never felt right using toilets with 50 other people together. Back home at Nankipooh, we had a one-hole outhouse, but at least it had privacy.That night, I had all the bathrooms to myself -- and I just knew I'd done gone to heaven.

They all came back the next day and basic training went about as usual, with people poking fun at me and everyone making me do push-ups and sit-ups. It wasn't long before this same private barged in accusing me of ratting out Sgt. Jones and getting him relieved. This private that I hardly knew started hitting me and calling me a Georgia cracker. I grabbed him and we fell to the ground scuffling. I ended up on his back with my legs around his waist and my arms under his chin, choking him. He didn't know I had been pulling a cross-cut saw and chopping wood all my life.

After they pulled me off him, I had to report to the orderly room. The first sergeant said I'd nearly choked the other guy to death and made it clear this had better be my last fight.

But they didn't make fun of me anymore. Not where I could hear them, anyway.

One day, two sharp-looking sergeants showed up with spit-shined jump boots and tailored clothes. It certainly got my attention. We were told they were the men we needed to speak with if we wanted to go airborne. Only about 10 of us out of the entire company went down to see them. My base pay at the time was $54 a month and they told me I could get paid another $55 if I jumped out of an airplane once a month. That was a no-brainer. I wasn't a genius, but I knew then I was going to double my pay.

I signed up for airborne and went from basic training to the Advanced Individual Training (AIT) with the 82nd Airborne Division, where they called us the 505 Panther Battalion.

They immediately got a hold of me and rode me down during the second AIT. Privates made me do push-ups and sit-ups. When sergeants, officers or really anybody else saw me they let me hear it.

"Get down Bragg."

"Push Bragg away."

"I hate Bragg."

I had the wrong name to be at Ft. Bragg, especially to go through jump school. But I was gaining muscle weight from regular meals and exercise. The flack given to trainees didn't always stick to words, however.

We were expected to be at parade rest when standing in the morning chow line. When somebody moves up, you come to attention, take a step forward and go back to parade rest. Then you'd stand there until the guy in front of you moves on. They had a pull-up bar at the chow hall and you were supposed to do three pull-ups to get in there. There were a pair of sergeants who thought they were bad that would stand and scream at us while we were in the chow line. We were all scared to death of those boys. One time they really got on the case of this one guy who didn't say much of anything. They were telling him to do this and that, get down, get up, and do it again. He finally reached a point where he stopped -- and they said they were going to whoop him.

"No, you won't whoop me," I remember him responding to the sergeants, who were both bigger than him.

One promised to teach him a lesson after chow. Uh oh. We just knew they were going to beat him up. We got upstairs in the barracks and here came the sergeants, calling for him.

"Come here, get in this room. I'm going to whoop you good," one of them yelled.

The other sergeant stood guard at the door, while his friend took the private in the room.

"Don't open this door for nobody. I'm going to teach this private a lesson."

The drill sergeant stood at the door while we heard all kind of noise in there. Wall lockers turning over. Bunks turning over. Hollering, screaming, banging and booming and carrying on. Then you heard a voice.

"Open the door!"

"I ain't opening the door for you, private. You can take that whoopin'," the drill sergeant grumbled.

"It's me," was the meek reply.

He opened the door and, sure enough, the private walked out and went to his bunk. Those two drill non-commissioned officers (NCOs) closed the door as they used a first aid kit to patch up the loser.

We were surprised. That little ol' boy didn't look like he could beat anybody in a fight. He must have been a wrestler or something back in high school, because he taught that drill sergeant a lesson -- and taught the rest of us a lesson, too: We all need to stand up a little bit more, a little straighter, because people who do a lot of talking can't do much else. We called it "wolfin'" in the Army.

"Sometimes he's just wolfin. That's all he's doing is hollering like a wolf, because they ain't no fight or there isn't a real wolf out there."

After going through jump school, I found myself standing as the second man in the door on a C-119. Folks once said the C-119 would

44

not fly, but Albert Einstein drew a bunch of numbers on a wall board and said it would. That was good enough for everyone else.

But it didn't really want to fly. When a C-119 went down the airstrip, the wings would actually start flapping up and down. It was a cargo plane, but it was our basic plane we jumped out of when I was a paratrooper. It wasn't the only plane we jumped, but the C-130 had a door on both sides and the rear of the plane could be opened.

When a red light came on you had 20 minutes to give jump commands. A guy name Blankenship from Kentucky was the first one on my side. They told us to stand at the opening door, with him in the lead waiting for the green light to signal time to go. The jump master began hitting him on the behind. Blankenship looked at me, who was already scared to death.

"I've never been in an airplane before in my life," he admitted to me.

"You ain't by yourself. I ain't never been in no airplane before, either." The green light came on. Blankenship jumped and I did too. It just wasn't gracefully as I'd hoped. I flipped around upside down and sideways, twisting my risers so badly I barely got untwisted before I hit the ground.

At the landing I watched the other boys were running around, hollering and jumping up and down.

"I'm airborne, I'm airborne. It's wonderful!"

I didn't see what was so wonderful. All I did was try to get untied on the way down. I must not have had a good body position when I jumped out of the plane. They put us right back on another plane for another round. The next jump went much smoother. I had the right position with my body and I looked up and the chute was over me. There wasn't any panic. I glanced ahead to see forever around me amid total quiet. It was serene, going from the aircraft propellers shooting noise back there to simply quiet. It was so beautiful.

We made five jumps. That first one was called your cherry jump. You'd get your Blood Wings after you get five jumps. They gave us two weeks leave after that.

I went back to Nankipooh. I was a paratrooper. Airborne. I went over to Hog Cash Grocery, geared up with my jump boots, fatigue britches and a T-shirt. (Because drill instructors liked to walk around a lot with T-shirts on.) I got a big RC Cola and a Moonpie and sat in the front of Hog Cash Grocery to look outside at the home I missed. Two cars went by in about 30 minutes, then I had a realization.

"I don't know what in the world I was homesick for. There ain't nobody here in Nankipooh."

When leave ended in December 1956, I went to the Brooklyn Army-Navy terminal and boarded the William O. Darby troop ship with what seemed to be 10 million other privates. I don't really know how many of us there were, but we were all headed to Germany. I think everyone on the ship was sick for the first three days. It happened to be my first time on a ship, too. They put me on a laundry detail using massive washing machines and dryers. That's where I worked for about two weeks until we arrived at Bremerhaven, Germany.

We went through disembarkation, whatever that means, and got on a train to Munich. Another train took us overnight to another location. The next morning I awoke and looked at an alien place through the window. There was someone driving a little bitty three-wheel truck. The other German cars were small, too. That was just the beginning. It was sort of a shock to see all these differences from America.

"We're in another world over here."

CHAPTER 3 -- A ROLLING RUCKUS THROUGH GERMANY

Munich was a wonderfully odd place. You could see a complete block of German buildings still blown out from 1945. Then, just down the road you would find a block of new buildings. One area was an old war zone, the other was new development. The United States helped rebuild Europe after the second World War, which is a contradiction for most world powers in history. When most conquered, they plundered, but not America. Whomever we defeated ended up better, like Japan.

I got to the 502nd and 503rd Airborne battle groups while still processing my culture shock. The two groups were housed in a six-story concern with miles of hallways. Each company received 20 to 50 new guys.We were the first replacements our boys had received in two years, but there was no grand welcome from the old guard.

Those men screamed at us from the windows as we marched. They yelled like they wanted to kill us, threatening to beat us up. I was scared to death. We were all scared to death. I didn't realize Americans did that to Americans, but we were newbies and they were the old guys. They put the fear of God in us and treated us roughly for the first year or so.

I became a 3.5 gunner in the third platoon, a weapons squad. In my earliest time there, they pulled most of my teeth on top because of cavities. They didn't give me a bridge or anything like that for a solid year, so I spent a good while in Germany without most of my teeth. Not surprisingly, I continued to be a target of ridicule during that time. They placed me on all kind of details, being the idiot of the unit. It was just a continuation of basic training and jump school harassment. Everybody from PFCs to Spec-4's and sergeants made me do push-ups and sit-ups.

I saw no need to go to town as a snaggletooth with few teeth, so I pulled guard duty or other details for soldiers on special weekends. They got to enjoy the nightlife by paying me $5 or $10 to stay there at the concern and work, which I did quite a bit.

A fellow asked if I'd pull a detail one weekend because it was time to refurbish headquarters' floors by buffing and waxing it again. They did this at night so they didn't have to close HQ.

I forget how much he paid me, but it wasn't important. I loved to run that buffer. Those machines are heavy and powerful. If you don't know how to raise the handle and keep the buffer spinning, it'll sling you around. Buffing a floor like that is an art. This rounded machine with handle spins and sands the floor just right if you know what you're doing.

I was there around 11 p.m. buffing the whole headquarters while the other guys on detail stood around talking and passing time. Unbeknownst to us, a sergeant major in civilian clothes passed through and observed us. The next night we waxed the floors. When I arrived at my company Monday, I discovered the 503rd Airborne battle group sergeant major had given me a three-day pass because I had worked harder than the other guys. That was my approach to doing most things. I couldn't just stand around. I was used to hard work even when no one else wanted to take it on.

The guy for whom I covered so he could run off to town was upset he missed out on the three-day pass. He claimed he should have it because it was his detail that he paid me for. It seems like I always had some friends help me out and vouch to him that not everyone on the detail got a pass. Honestly, this fellow probably would have been one of those standing around talking.

Things started to change after a year in Germany as part of the 503rd Rock, 11th Airborne Division. They gave me a dental bridge, so when I looked in the mirror and smiled, I finally had teeth! I was still a teenager, but I was becoming a man. I woke up one day weighing 240 pounds and able to do 100 sit-ups, 100 push-ups and then run 20 miles. I didn't realize all them boys making me do push-ups and sit-ups were actually molding my body into something better. And I looked good, too. That's when I got confidence in myself -- and began acting up. I started going to town regularly and getting in all kinds of fights.

I remember around that time we did a combat jump outside Copenhagen, Denmark. It was hard to take in that we were jumping in over the Baltic Sea and landing right outside the city before getting to go to town. Europe is truly a beautiful place to see and the same goes for the pretty women there. We once took a three-day pass to Paris, France. I signed up for a USO Club trip.

Though I'd been adjusting to life abroad, there were some things I couldn't get used to seeing. I was shocked there were prostitutes lined up every 50 feet on some streets. Coming from South Georgia, that was absolutely an oddity. Many buildings in Paris were so old and unkempt that you'd get filthy walking down the street sometimes. The most dangerous thing was trying to cross streets at roundabouts. There were no lanes for traffic to stay within. People just went in whichever way they wanted to get around the circle. It always looked like drivers were going to run over you when you stepped out. I believe some of them were trying to hit us, being Americans. We were lucky each time we made it across the street.

The 11th Airborne was eventually deactivated because so many people were getting in fights with and killing Germans. If you were on guard duty and shot a fella trying to jump the fence to go to town, then you'd get to go back to the United States. So then they took live ammunition away from guards and gave us pick-handles. That way if someone jumped the wall, you'd only beat them up with pick-handles -- and get to come back to the States. Homesickness made us a bit foolish. We didn't appreciate that we were in Europe, best place in the world for vacation, but we were there trying to get back to America.

They moved a few of us paratroopers about 50 miles away to Augsburg, Germany when they deactivated 11th Airborne. I think that was the 24th infantry division. There was such a distinct difference between paratroopers and regular soldiers. Paratroopers had spit-shine boots and tailored clothes and block hats. We were proud of ourselves. Regular soldiers did the minimum they could do, with ragley, sloppy uniforms and they never shined their boots. They didn't show the same pride.

During my time in Augsburg, I met a private named Pickren from Pooka Wonka, South Dakota. He received a federal check for $800 as an American Indian. He got with me and a buddy of mine, named Jones. Jones was from Two Egg, Alabama and I, of course, was from Nankipooh. Pickren told us he wanted to go on a three-day pass so we could spend that federal money he'd gotten. He only took about $300, but we were still surprised that he received so much money from the government for who he was.

We used our pass to return to old stomping grounds in Munich. We only decided what we were going to do when we arrived at the bahnhof rail station. Jones said he wanted to go with as many women or prostitutes as he could during that time. Pickren said he wanted to see how many fights he could get in. I chose to see how long I could stay awake and drink beer.

We ventured down from a bahnhof in an area known as Pig Alley to the Dolly Bar. The night started with few drinks and agreement to meet back at the bar Saturday morning at 10 o'clock to see how we were doing with our missions. I got back to the Dolly Bar when time came, after sneaking a nap or two in during the wee hours of the morning, but I didn't tell my buddies. Pickren arrived with his shirt torn and knots on his head, bragging he had been in three fights. Jones strutted in bragging how he had bedded five women. I think all three of us were lying.

Our reunion was brief before splitting up again with plans to meet back at Dolly Bar at 10 a.m. Sunday. I was out all night from place to place and frankly, I don't remember all I did do. Pickren came in and his left coat sleeve was nearly torn off. He'd been in a good scuffle because he had lots of bruises around the head and neck, but he was happy and he thought he was doing well, now having made it through eight fights. Jones came around moping and looked so pitiful I couldn't believe it. We hung around a while and dispersed again.

That was Sunday and we had to be back at reveille Monday morning at 0600 hours. We decided to meet later at bahnhof at midnight. The last train left going to Augsburg at 1 a.m. By Sunday afternoon, the guys said I walked out of the bathroom with my britches around my ankles at the Columbus bar. They took me to a booth and tried to get my clothes on before I got thrown out of the bar.

I also met up with some old friends still stationed in Munich. They laughed about how messed up and crazy I was. We headed out to the Dixie Bar that evening around 8 o'clock. About three or four of my buddies were carrying me along because I was kind of staggering around by this point. When we got there, everybody was outside looking in through the windows and doors. There must be a terrible fight at the Dixie Bar, we thought. People were hot about it, jumping up to try to get a peek over the crowd. Just look at them!

"That boy's crazy!" a voice said. "He's messed in his britches and now he's reaching in his britches to get manure and sling it at folks!"

I finally got a glimpse at this wild man captivating the crowd. It was Jones, my boy from Two Egg, Alabama. He was turning around and around just a slinging. He had cleared the bar, except for one person sitting at a table. That, of course, was Pickren, who was about to die laughing at Jones' antics.

We eventually got Jones settled down and a fella who was on leave took him to a hotel with extra clothes and washed him. Management had run us out of the bar, so we got ourselves back to the bahnhof between 11-12 p.m. None of us were in good shape, but we were able to order a goulash soup. It was a Hungarian soup that was good, but you wouldn't believe how good that goulash soup was after that night out on the town. Jones and I ate our soup quickly. We noticed Pickren hadn't touched his soup. Around this time his head was falling forward into the bowl, we grabbed the bowl and let his head hit the table, then we sort of fought over his soup.

It was a challenge to get those boys on the train going back because I could hardly stay awake. Pickren and Jones were sprawled out on the floor like they were passed out. I begged the conductor, a German comrade -- we then called Germans comrades -- to make sure we didn't pass Augsburg, even if he had to throw us off the train.

After arriving in Augsburg, comrade helped me roll those two scoundrels off the train onto the platform. I think comrade enjoyed kicking and pushing them off the train because we were rather rude Americans. (I'm honestly ashamed of that period of my life, for being so wild and crazy.) We fumbled about to get inside a cab. We were in a crunch to get to the back end of the Sheridan Concern. You couldn't go in the front gate after bed check at 10 o'clock, but we knew a place in the back where you could climb the wall. It had three strands of barbed wire at the top of the wall, but so many guys had gone over it they had mashed that razor wire down and tore down the barbed wire where it wasn't so bad.

These weren't normal circumstances, considering my and my pals' condition. In getting both of them over that 7-foot brick wall to the other side, we were cut up something fierce by that barbed wire and razor wire, but I think we had about an hour until 6 o'clock reveille. If we missed that, we were going to be in even more trouble.

I could hear the whole battalion falling into formation as we walked out of the bushes. I had Jones on one side and Pickren on another and we were staggering up behind the formation. I was hollering to get their attention, just before the man reported us AWOL. When they finally saw us, we fell on the ground and reported that we made it. Sgt. Schwab had us carried to the upstairs shower in the barracks. They ran water over us, fully clothed, and left us there. We finally crawled around on our own and got into bed.

Now that was the roughest three-day pass I've ever heard of or can remember anybody telling me that they went on in the history of the United States Army. I don't know how we survived or how we got back.

I'd been in Germany close to two-and-a-half years when I started going to the EM Club on the Sheridan Concern. The Army had integrated by this time, but we were having some racial problems and some fights. I came out of the EM Club one night with a guy named Hardwick. We'd been inside moments before telling each other how bad we were, since we were both pretty big boys. As we walked outside the EM Club, three guys come up and started talking smack. I knew they were going to jump on us. They didn't wait long.

Hardwick just kept on walking and I found myself fighting off these three guys. I poked one in the eyes. The other two ran away when the SPs (Security Patrol -- they weren't MPs but they patrolled inside the Sheridan Concern.) drove up in a jeep. I was glad the guys who attacked me were gone, but I was confounded by the SPs doing nothing about it.

"What are you doing?" I asked them. "You're sitting down there half a block away and they're up here jumping on people."

I left walking again looking for Hardwick. I was going to fight him because he walked off and left me to fend for myself.

I made it down by a gym, walking over snow and ice covering the rough cobblestone roads. Out of nowhere, one of those guys after me earlier grabbed me around the back of my head. I swear I don't know how he snuck up on me. Another one came running around the building, but I slung him by the shoulders and didn't see him anymore.

The other man still had me around the back of my head as I twisted and turned. I struggled, but finally grabbed him under his knees and pulled his legs up to my chest, while he was somehow still on the back on my head. I stood with this man on me in a contorted position, with his knees on my stomach, before he finally he slid off back-first onto the cobblestone. Now it was my turn.

I started kicking him. I'd gotten the one I really wanted. I knew I had him. And he had it coming. There wasn't a way for him to get away from me and I was going to beat him to death. I booted him a few more times, walked around and told him how bad I was going to hurt him. I kicked him some more until, in a flash, he was on his feet and moving. There wasn't any way I could catch him. I had let him get away after his buddies and he jumped me two times in the same night.

I didn't know exactly who they were, but they had beat up other guys outside of EM Club and jumped on their chest. Two or three guys were hospitalized in critical condition like they were going to die. It was an ongoing battle.

I turned again to go find Hardwick. When I ran by the NCO club, this other guy told me my three assailants were from D Company. I should have jumped on him and whooped him because he must have seen the whole thing or some of it. Hardwick and he could have made it a fair fight if they would have helped me.

My next steps went straight to D Company, where I looked up to the windows by a stairway and one of these guys who jumped me was going up the steps. I sprinted up the steps and saw him at the other end of the hallway. I was on restriction in my company, where I wasn't even supposed to be out of my company in the first place.

So, naturally, I ran down the hall and jumped on him. Everybody in the company knew him, so they got in the middle and separated us. I told them I owed this guy for jumping me outside the EM Club. The CQ (charge of quarters guard) knew I wasn't from that company and demanded I leave. Even as I walked back to my company, the thought of what happened to me only made me angrier. That made my mind up for me.

"I'm going to go back over there and pull bed check on that guy."

"Bed check" is when you beat somebody up while they're asleep. I turned to the company that just told me to leave. I stormed in, slinging open the squad bay door and turning on the lights. About 10 surprised men were staring at me. None of them were the one I wanted. I turned the light off and went to the next room to continue my search. The CQ returned and ran me out again. That only postponed my hunt.

The next day I went to our consolidated mess hall where the entire battalion eats. I stood in at the door waiting for one or all three to show up so I could settle the score. Word must have traveled fast, because they never came to eat. I was upset and disappointed, but my biggest problem didn't happen until later that day.

And you know it's some kind of problem when urine and waste starts leaking from your navel.

It continued to ooze from my stomach the rest of the evening. The next morning I was on sick call. There was a German doctor who examined me. He said he knew what was wrong and told me to grab my shaving kit and tell everyone else I was going to be at the hospital for a while. I got there only to find out they were planning surgery. Being the big, strong boy I was I thought if they operated tomorrow, I'd be out the day after. Hospital staff assured me I couldn't, but I was certain I would.

The surgeon sliced me from my navel down as far as he could go. I still have quite the scar to remember that. They said I had busted my gut and the urine and waste was in my stomach. I guessed I hurt myself when I picked up one of my attackers a couple days earlier. The operation was successful, but I didn't feel too well afterward. Matter of fact, I didn't feel like anything.

I laid in bed, but I didn't eat much more than a little bit of food. Any time someone came to talk I'd roll away in bed and look at the wall. That's how bad I felt. I don't know if I was there a day or two or or a week. One afternoon, I sat up on the bed and that urine and waste started coming out the stitch hole. Some guys got a towel and tried to catch it with that. There was so much, one of them tried using a bed sheet.

They went down the hall to get a doctor and nurse. The doctor grabbed my bed into the hallway and put me in another room across the hall. He got a scalpel and cut my scar tissue open from navel down as far as he could go. He told the nurse to make me lie down because I was sitting up watching him cut me open. Next thing I knew, I was out, again. I think I woke up the next day or so, when I noticed they had packed my stomach full of gauze. I was bed-ridden, but I didn't feel anything like I did before. Someone would come everyday to remove my stomach gauze and repack it with a new one. They wanted it to heal from the inside and told me I was on strict bed rest until then.

But if I raised up a little bit, the incision would come open and you could look down in my stomach. Word spread about this new "talent" and people around wanted to come see it. I saw opportunity.

I started charging a dollar each to look in the hole and curiosity spread. More and more kept coming. I set a rate of a dollar per person to look in the hole or $2 for three.

Feeling the entrepreneurial spirit, I recalled a guy that used to be in my room who had a drawing kit he bought from the PX at the bottom floor of the hospital. If you stayed in the line with that water color kit, it would produce a beautiful picture. I was fascinated when I saw how easy it made drawing, so I got one and started making illustrations. When people came to look at my hole, they'd see the pictures I was selling for $5 a piece. They asked me if I was an artist.

"Yea, I'm a pretty good artist. I took art school at Nankipooh High School," I would reply. (Nankipooh didn't have a high school. Nankipooh just went to the seventh grade.)

Thankfully I didn't need art training to draw a beautiful photo thanks to that kit, even if I was having to be a bit sneaky at times. The captain and the nurse had told me not to get out of bed, because I was known to go standing against the door frame and look up the hallway. I was used to PT (Physical Training) and working. It was just killing me to stay in bed. The nursed warned me if I got caught out of bed again, she was would press charges against me.

One day when I was behaving, staying in bed and sleeping -- because business was slow, some guys arrived and woke me up to look in the hole and buy some pictures. I arose to give them a look in the hole and laid down after they bought some drawings. This one fellow was later brought in with his hand wrapped up, apparently cutting it after punching through a window. I saw he had a big gauze on his hand as he rested in another bed in the room. He looked back at me, paused and said, "Country?" I finally recognized my new roommate as the man they called Big Ass Herrin from Atlanta. Big Herrin was a bad character, badder than me -- and I thought I was a big, bag man.

"You look like a ghost," he pointed out while asking what I'd been doing. I had lost a lot of weight, down from 240 pounds to about 160-170 pounds. I was a skeleton and pale as a ghost. I'd been in the hospital almost two months. After pointing out how pitiful I looked, Herrin asked to look in the hole among my sutures.

"That'll be a dollar," I said.

"Don't give me that crap, Country. I ain't paying you no dollar to look in your hole."

"Then you ain't looking."

Herrin wondered if I really drew the pictures I sold. I told him yes and sold him one. Then I told him it was a kit. I had even set up a system where another guy in the room drew them for me and I'd give him $2 from each $5 picture I'd sell. I kept the most since I had the concession going by bringing people in who wanted to see into my stomach. The nurse had told me to stop because she wasn't going to put up with that mess. Too many people coming in there visiting. I had been running them in and out as quick as I could.

Despite the nurse's crackdown, Herrin decided he wanted to go exploring. He told me to put on my hospital gown because we were going down to the PX to get a coloring kit so he could get into the picture-drawing business.

"Look, Herrin I can't do that. I'm on strict bed rest and they're already on my case," I tried to reason. "I've been in trouble. They're going to court martial me or do something to me."

"Put on that gown and come on," Herrin said.

I knew I shouldn't have done what Big Herrin told me to do, but I went along with him. (I told you I was a confirmed idiot, getting into every bit of trouble I could.) I had been in that ward almost two months, but here we were in the hall going to the PX. We got on an elevator to go downstairs.

The elevator of the four-story building was having work done, so its ceiling had been removed, exposing an I-beam just above our heads.

"You can't even do a pull-up you're in so bad a shape," Herrin said.

I felt up to his challenge. I grabbed the I-beam and tried to do a pull-up, but in my moment of triumph the elevator went down and left me hanging on the beam. I yelled to Herrin that I was going to fall.

"I can't hold on. I'm slipping!"

"Hang on, I'm coming! I'm coming!"

Herrin's ride stopped on the first or second floor. As he was ready to come to the rescue, the elevator door opened as a nun, my nurse and the captain who had threatened me with punishment walked in. I didn't know who got on the elevator, but I knew I was in a tight spot as it was coming up. I held on until it was one floor away from reaching me, but my weakened body gave out. My hands slipped from off that I-beam and I fell. Herrin was about 6'5" and weighed about 270. Good thing he was also a big boy. He caught me, but I knocked him to the floor.

As I'm lying on top in his arms, I look up and there's the captain and a nun. They had Herrin pick me up, since my body was as limp as water, and put me in bed. The captain and the nurse, who had been so friendly with me -- I just knew she liked me -- pulled my bed down the hallway to another room with nothing inside but a radiator under the window. She locked the door and I spent the rest of my time in the hospital inside a locked room with a bedpan. It didn't seem long after that my hole healed and they released me from the hospital.

My hair had grown long by the time I could go back to my company, now in Hohenfels, Germany. That is a training area in a rough place you didn't want to go. It had desolate, bombed out terrain. I talked to the guy they left there to answer the phone. He said the company wouldn't be back for a week, but I couldn't do anything anyway because I was restricted to light duty for a month. I couldn't strain at all because my incision might burst open. I asked him for and received a pass from the first sergeant's book to go to town.

Elvis Presley had been stationed in northern Germany around that time and he was going to be in Munich or Augsburg that weekend. I put on my little suit coat and went downtown to the Atlantic Bar, just to have something to do, because I was in a weakened condition. I walked in around 9 o'clock, with all that long hair -- when they were expecting Elvis might show up. Suddenly, girls flocked to me at the door, mistaking me for The King. It didn't take them long to realize just because I had long hair, I wasn't Elvis.

That was about the end of my excitement in Germany, aside from a few minor hiccups in behavior. I'd certainly made an impression. This big Alaskan sergeant, Swatay was his name, told me I caused him so much trouble that he was going to get a brass band to play for me to show how happy he was to see me leave the country.

Nope. Tommy Bragg didn't cause any more trouble in Germany, but I was still getting into mischief. It just happened to be at sea.

We were aboard a ship for a nine-day trip across the Atlantic Ocean to the Brooklyn Army Naval Terminal in New York. I met a guy who had married a German prostitute and was taking her back home to New Orleans. Unfortunately, he wasn't thinking of a new life of wedded bliss. This fellow said he planned for his bride to keeping working as a prostitute to make him plenty of money. He was a slick talker. I remember this cool little rhyme he often used: "If you ain't hip, you got to get off this ship."

This soldier and his buddy later approached me to be a front man for some on-board gambling. They wanted to pay me $100 a night to stand at the door while they rolled dice. I didn't have to think long to take an easy job paying that kind of money. They would go down in the bottom of the ship in different compartments and put down a blanket where they would roll dice. I wasn't aware at the time that bossman was cheating the competition, somehow switching the dice in his hand. All I knew was that I was supposed to stand there and watch from the doorway and if someone showed up and saw them in the act, I'd block the interloper long enough to give everyone else a head start out another door.

No one ever caught on to their operation. It was easy money, but it was coming from my two new buddies on the boat who were just natural criminals. I was just stupid.

We'd been on the ship a day or two when I was assigned to guard duty on the deck where the soldiers were. Guys were in shorts with their shirts off getting a tan, except for me. One of these hooligans I was buddying started pressuring me to join them.

"What are you guarding? You think someone's going to sneak up in this whole ocean and on this boat? You look so stupid standing there with that little white hat on and that stick.

"Take off your shirt and get yourself a tan. You've been in Germany three years and you look like a ghost."

Moments later I'd put down my hat and stick, removed my shirt and was lying down to bask in the sunshine. I barely got settled in before I heard another voice asking who owned the helmet and stick on the deck. Everybody on deck pointed to me.

It was the second-in-command on the ship, a Navy XO (executive officer) and two other Navy guys. The XO ordered the guy who convinced me to goof off to get dressed and fill in for me until a replacement guard arrived. The officer took me downstairs for a fierce chewing out. It was stupid of me to try tanning when I knew guard duty was serious business. (But, seriously, who's going to slip up on a ship?)

It didn't get any better for me.

Our ship made a two-day stop in Rhoda, Spain to pick up about 300 Marines, which delayed our voyage back to New York. There may have been some foreshadowing about more trouble when I woke up from sleeping in my hammock. Crews had been unloading the ship where my hammock was. I was a bit startled to see they had removed the deck floor on each level past my bunk. It was at least 100 feet from my hammock to the belly of that ship. I could have fallen out and died right then. Instead, I slipped out safely as my two new "friends" informed me we were going to town. That's a problem when you're not supposed to leave the ship.

"All we have to do is go upstairs, get in line and sign off with the dependents. They won't know we're soldiers," one of them reassured me.

So we put on slacks and shirts and made it through the line just as planned. Each of us signed our name as "Roy Rogers." It was slick and it worked. At least, until we started walking down beside the gangplank. That's when some of the guys on the ship recognized us and started hollering that we weren't supposed to be out there.

We sprinted away and got into a cab, making out getaway over a hill. The boys took me to a bar around 11 o'clock. Our time was limited since the ship was leaving in about four hours. We went in this bar because there was hardly anyone there. The two guys found two working girls and went to the back room for some private time. They egged me to go, too, saying they had plenty of money to pay my way, but I wasn't interested in messing with a prostitute.

They later finished up their time and we started walking to another bar up the hill. That's when we saw this beautiful girl come walking down the street wearing a large flowery dress that made her look like a Flamenco dancer. She walked past us. I kept going a few steps and stopped. Those boys stopped as she passed to turn around and watch her while I kept going. She stopped and came back, walking past them only to grab me by the arm. She took me to a house around the corner, then she guided me to the bedroom where we started making love. That sounds crazy, but that showed me that the new dental bridge I had was working out fine.

During fascia (a time of partying for Germans) all the other soldiers went back for bed check at 10 p.m., but not me. I'd walk the streets of Munich until I came upon the Hopenhouse (a large hall) where Germans were having a big time.

I went in and joined a real party. It was not long until a real good looking girl started sittin in my lap and kissing me. Next thing I know, we are down the street at 2 or 3 a.m. in the snow and ice, fifteen degrees below zero, making out on the hood of a Volkswagen car. Somehow, she became stuck to the car. I had to warm up the car from the outside to get her loose. I really enjoyed it but she disappeared in the snow as soon as she got free.

Back to Spain: We came out of the house only to realize we soldiers were about to miss our ride back to the States. We got into the taxi and arrived at the ship as the horn was blowing as they pulled up the gangplank. We boarded hastily and forgot to salute the captain and XO as we arrived. Next thing I know we're being chased around the ship. I snuck away long enough to get my khaki uniform on before going back up and relieving the on-duty guard. My pursuers were running right past me, looking for me, while I was on guard duty. I couldn't seem to get away from trouble and my luck would run out.

A few days later I was on daytime guard duty on the dependant deck during a cold, drizzling rain when a woman wearing a big fur coat stopped by. We talked for quite a bit and she talked about my plight being stuck in such dreary weather.

"You're going to catch a cold," she said. "It's terrible they make you stand out here like this."

"Well it's guard duty and you have to pull guard duty," I explained. "I'll be out there tonight at the same place from 2-4. That's where it's going to get rough, cold and windy."

When I returned for my later guard duty, I sat in a deck chair on the dependant level, carefully positioned in the shadows where I couldn't be seen too easily. Soon after, a door opened and she walked out wearing that big fur coat she always had on. Then she got in the deck chair with me. It wasn't long before I knew I was in trouble again.

We were well into what we were doing and that same skinny Navy officer barged through the door and started screaming at her. I mean he was mad at her. He told her to get to her apartment and he would deal with her later for fraternizing with an enlisted man on guard. Then he and a couple of other Navy guys took me in and gave me the Navy general orders -- which are unbelievably long -- for a ship and told me I had to learn them by heart by the next day.

The officer put me on meals of bread and water and took me to the nose of the ship where he placed me in the brig. There were two cells there made out of iron bars right in the ship's nose. It was nasty, cold and dark. The only lights were the lights on the side of the ship. It made a creaky noise and other weird sounds down there with all the stuff stored at the bottom of that boat. I nearly froze to death staying that night. It was unbelievably the wrong place to be. I don't know if I stayed in there two days or three, because you didn't know if it was light of day or dark, which blurred times together.

After days of steady bread and water meals, a master chief arrived with two Navy guys -- and a full meal. He asked how I was doing, talking nicely.

"Well, I'm not getting in any trouble since I've been in this cage."

"I'm going to let you out of this thing tomorrow so you can see the Statue of Liberty," he said, assuring me I would get regular food until then.

"You're not thinking about committing suicide?"

"No, I don't reckon I'll do that," I told him. "But I could use a blanket because I'm freezing to death."

Even in my situation, I was worried about the woman because that officer was so mad at her. The master chief said she was staying with the captain now. Every time you saw the captain, you saw her. She even dined with the captain. Someone told me how she got on the ship and how she put that officer down when he made a play for her. It now made sense why he got so enraged when he saw her with me. Even though she was doing wrong, he still overreacted.

My incarceration finally ended as the Statue of Liberty came into view. Upon arrival in New York, they sent me to Ft. Jackson in South Carolina where they discharged me after three years in the Army. I'd gone from a complete idiot, bald head with cavity teeth to a healthy 230-pound man with nothing but muscle and a real pretty bridge across the front of my mouth. I also accumulated six Article 15 reprimands in Germany, three each in two places. It's a miracle they didn't throw me out, since three Article 15's is enough to warrant that.

I don't know how I survived all that trouble in my first three years in the Army. I was just looking for excitement and I had no fear. I was a good soldier now. As long as I stayed in the field, I was excellent. My squad leaders and platoon leaders loved me, but things changed when I went to town. I was a country boy without the social skills for living in a big world. Growing up in Nankipooh, I never got out much, never went to a party. That's why I think I stayed in such a terrible mess those three years.

I was bigger than most guys and didn't look too bad, either. Girls liked me, but the downside to talking with them came when they found out how stupid I was. It didn't take them long to figure me out. Things went from, "You're so big and strong and good-looking!" to "You make me sick!" about an hour or two later. That's how it went once they saw what was in my head.

After exiting the Army I took a Greyhound bus to Nankipooh. The bus was heading to the station in Columbus, so I asked the driver to let me off on the side of the highway and I walked two miles from there carrying a duffle bag to get home. My homecoming felt like a grand occasion. All my brothers and sisters were there and excited to see me back. My mother had some friends over, so we had a party.

I came back to Nankipooh with brighter hopes than when I left. I had grown, maybe matured a little bit, and I had saved a decent amount of money so I could do something after I left the service.

At least I thought I had.

Not long after coming home, I learned my mother had spent all the money I'd sent home, except for three government bonds not yet old enough to cash. When I asked what happened, she admitted she'd actually sent it to some other fella.

All that money, including what I earned from pulling all those extra details for people, was gone. I wasn't just mad. I was crushed.

The next morning I took what little pay I had, about $200 or $300, and stayed drunk for the next two weeks to deal with the depression. I would pass out in bars, wake up the next day only to lay around or sleep on someone's couch until I went back to drinking. That didn't leave me in the best mood and it seemed like I'd fought just about everyone in town.

During my wandering I met a guy named Ruit "Red" Fuller. He was notorious. He had cut a lot of people and had been in prison. He came into a bar where I was already hanging out. The waitress warned me to go to another bar to avoid this terrible character. He was a big guy with a bad reputation as a ruffian and thug. It wasn't long before me and Red Fuller started fighting. We kept at it until we both got so tired that we quit. I actually stayed at his house that night. He was renting a room on the back of a house, but it was the worst dump you ever saw. Yet I stayed there because I didn't have anywhere else to go.

We drank for a week or so together. It was an eye-opening experience. I'd never been around anyone like that who was just plain out mean and rough. All he lived for was to get drunk, fight and act a fool. After a couple of weeks I woke up one day hungry, broke and with a few knots on my head. I knew that's not how I wanted to live.

The Army had been the only meal-ticket I'd known, so I walked to the recruiting office in Columbus to re-enlist to go in the Army. My troubles nearly kept me out for good this time. I had been a PFC (private first class) for three years after having my rank busted a few times. Most people are sergeants after that time. The recruiter called jump school, in Ft. Benning and they told him they didn't need a three-year PFC and they have enough duds already.

The recruiter asked what I thought about joining the Rangers. I was up for that. In my prior service, everybody talked about how tough it was being a Ranger. He called the Ranger department. The person on the other end of the line asked if could run five miles?

"Yea, I can run five miles backwards," I said eagerly.

Then the person at Ranger department asked if I could fight. The recruiter looked my way and examined the swollen eyes, busted lips and knots on head I got from two weeks of drunken brawling.

"He'll fight, but I don't know if he can win."

CHAPTER 4 -- MAKING A RANGER
OUT OF A RASCAL

The Army recruiter gave me the good news. Ranger department wanted me to come over so they could look at me. It's hard to get into Ranger school in the first place.

I told the recruiter I need something to eat, but didn't have any money. He took me to main post for chow before going to meet Master Sgt. Joe Cason, who was in charge of the Ranger committee. Ranger department was at the back of Ft. Benning, in what they called Harmony Church, about 20 miles from Columbus.

The master sergeant asked where I was from. When I said Nankipooh, Georgia, he pointed out he was from Tupelo, Mississippi. After the small talk, he marched me to see Maj. Gouch, who was in charge of the Benning Training Committee and was really the one who had to accept me. We talked. We left and Master Sgt. Cason finally said the words I'd been waiting to hear, and then some.

"I'm recommending that we give you a chance and that you be assigned here until you go to Ranger school," he said, before reminding me of the favor I was getting. "But don't you ever turn on me. No matter what, you won't never turn." I assured him I wouldn't.

When I got to Ranger department they put me to work drilling holes for 2x6 boards with a brace and bit to run a 1" pipe through to build horizontal ladders, which looked like monkey bars from the playground. They were used for class training where you'd have to work your way across bar by bar with your hands while keeping your feet off the ground as part of the physical fitness test. They had about 15-16 lanes for the ladders and that meant there was a lot of holes to drill with a brace and bit. I went back to Nankipooh for a week or so about two months later at Christmas. My Ranger class would begin January of 1960.

They assigned me to a Ranger buddy named Max Haney. When you go to Ranger school, you go on buddy teams. You always had to watch out for each other whether you're in the woods at night or in the water. The buddy system was meant to lessen chances of a man getting lost, hurt or killed without anybody knowing where he is located. I was in Ranger Class 5 beginning vJanuary 7. Haney had been in the 11th Airborne in Germany and in Augsburg like I had been. He was a Spec-4, since he didn't get his rank busted like I did. Haney was a smart guy from Indiana. He was stocky and had a lot of common sense. He also graduated from high school, so I was very lucky to get with a guy like Max.

You have three weeks of intense training day and night at Ft. Benning, mostly physical fitness. Haney and I had 8 or 10 good spot reports at Ft. Benning and we burned through the compass course, which was a navigational course over about 10 miles traveled at night from one point to another, each stop with instructions to find another one. Max and I broke the record.

Then we made it to Florida ranger camp where we had a landing craft utility (LCU) training. This wasn't something you approached as just another class. Three ranger students drowned as a storm hit us as we were coming in to the Santa Rosa Sound. It disabled our landing craft and we had to get it to shore the best we could. That night I was the Company runner assigned to go along the beach and find any Rangers that had drowned or needed help. The storm eventually calmed enough so you could see pretty well in the light. As the waves washed in, I saw a body of a Ranger student floating. He still had on his life jacket and wet gear, but he was gone. All the blood had left his pale face. I dragged him up as far as I could on the beach. I left him there, remembering where he was, and continued down the beach looking for other rangers I could help out of the water. I met a Capt. Doogan, who had just pulled out another drowned Ranger. Doogan was a Ranger instructor and a real fine officer.

My platoon had landed farther down the beach and built a big fire in the sand dunes. They had forgotten I was assigned to Company headquarters and was serving as Company runner. They knew I was a weak swimmer and assumed I drowned or was lost at sea. When I made it to them, I was walking from the ocean to them. Some of them hollered when they saw me, then ran down and tackled me on the beach, happy to see I was still around.

Haney was assigned to Company radio operator on that mission. When we left Florida after that training at Eglin Air Force Base, Auxiliary Field 7, we came back to Ft. Benning on the way to the mountains in Dahlonega. On the board was orders making me a corporal. That was one way to be a corporal: if you were already a sergeant and got busted.

We got to mountain Ranger camp and one of the first missions we were assigned to was escape and evasion. We were to move through enemy lines and get back to friendly lines. They had aggressors throughout the mountains there. If we got on trails and roads, it was a sure thing we'd get caught or captured. You surely didn't want to get captured in escape and evasion because they would torture you like you were a POW. I told Haney we would not get captured, but we were also going to walk the road because it was easier and we had a long way to go.

We were coming around a dirt road curve on the side of the mountain. On the left side was the rock of the mountain side. To the right side was a 50 to 100 foot drop. As we came around the curve about 20 aggressors jumped out and ran toward us. There was no way to outrun them back down the road, so I just jumped off the side of the road and hit the ground about 50 feet down. I began bouncing and rolling over rocks, hitting bushes and mountain laurel all the way to the bottom where there was a dry stream bed. My weapon came down on top of me. I was afraid to move because I was just certain I had broke bones. Before I knew it, here comes Max bouncing down the mountain with rocks and gravel coming with him. He landed right beside me. I waited a few seconds before checking on him.

"You OK?"

"I'm not going to try to move," he said.

We were in the same predicament. Luckily, neither one had any broken bones or anything permanent. We were was just bruised and sore.

But we did not get captured.

We moved on and got back to our friendly lines. Some of the other Rangers got captured and got bad spot reports and write-ups.

Ranger school, being the toughest school in the U.S. Army, brings out the best in you or the worst in you. It's day and night and you have to function under great stress and make life-and-death decisions while you're under this stress with no rest or sleep after you've been moving and playing war.

After we ran our patrolling missions, Haney and I were taken up to Mt. Yonah. It was cold, freezing and Max and I were picked to be on the first belay team. We were to go up on the top of the mountain and tie ourselves into the mountain, then feed down 120-foot nylon climbing rope so the other part of the class would tie this rope around their waists about five times and tie it off. Then they would start climbing up the side of the mountain, using their hands and feet. If they slipped and fell, we would have the belay line under our left arm, around our back and in our right hand while leaning back against the mountain tied in, so we could just put our right arm across our chest and break their fall. That way they could get their fingers and toes into cracks and crevices and climb up to the top of the cliff.

While we were looking for a place to tie in, naturally I'm down looking over the cliff, where I shouldn't have been. Max had gone over trying to help two other Rangers trying to place the tie-in. There was a sheet of ice about 4-5 foot wide with grass growing in it where he was at. After that, it was solid ice coming down to the top of the cliff. It got to 20 feet wide where it went over the cliff. Max took 2-3 steps and slipped and fell back on the ice. At first he tried to grab hold of the ice with his hands and feet, but then he just turned around and was just sitting on the ice, sliding to the edge of the cliff.

I had not tied in myself so I was down there just looking and, before I knew it, he slid past me. I was able to grab the rope he had tied around his waist. I fell back against the cliff and Max nearly stopped. He was sitting with his behind right on the edge of the cliff with his arms and legs sticking out over space. Then he went on over and his full body weight was against me. I had the rope with both hands. Gradually I was moving forward and I was at the point where I had to make the decision to go with him and fall down about 90 feet to a ledge and then maybe 300-400 ft off a steep incline of loose rocks and gravel where they had blowed off the side of the mountain for us to train there. He would have surely died if he had fallen and bounced down the cliff. Just as I was getting ready to let him go or go with him, two other rangers come over and helped me pull him back up.

Max and I still disagree on one detail. He can't believe I held onto him without myself being tied into the mountain. Of course, since he was over the cliff, how could he see what I did?

Many years later at his birthday party in his house, he had about 20 children and family members there. He told them that same story and explained how if it had not been for me grabbing that rope, they probably wouldn't be here in his blood line.

After that we got back to Ft. Benning, where we found a roster on the board that made Max and me sergeants. They also asked us to stay there as Ranger instructors. The main thing they wanted me to do was be the hand-to-hand man. When we teach Ranger students hand-to-hand, we do demonstrations and we put on a tremendous hand-to-hand demos, where we actually throw and beat each other to get the effects. The Rangers do the same.

I took to it like a hog in slop. I demonstrated bayonets, demolitions, pugil sticks and patrolling. In one year I worked my way up to the number one hand-to-hand instructor. You would start off the number four man and work your way up, similar to working your way up to a black belt with Judo or Karate.

I was still a little wild and crazy, but I was Airborne, Ranger and Ranger instructor, even if I was living way out there in the Harmony church area with no car. One of the craziest things that happened while I was there came after meeting this character of a sergeant. After finishing Ranger school, I was in charge of this two-story second World War barracks with a little porch, 10x10 on the back side and front side of the building. I woke up and looked around and it was like a ghost town. All the Ranger students were gone. All the instructors lived in town and I lived in the barracks. It went from a complete carnival atmosphere with people going everywhere hollering and shouting to nobody being there. I walked outside the barracks and stood on the porch and looked up the company street.

"Oh my gracious!" I remember thinking. "I'm going to be out here in these woods 20 miles from town with no car. It's going to be a bad two or three years with no Ranger class here."

About that time I heard a door slam and I looked across the Company street and here came a fella dragging a duffle bag. He had his hat on cock-eyed sideways. His fatigue jacket was 3 or 4 sizes too big. He had a rocker with three stripes up with a "T" in it. I had never seen what they call a tech sergeant. His boots were half-laced up and half-bloused. I wondered, "What kind of animal is this?

As he got closer to me, I saw he had been hit with White Phosphorus in Korea and it had burned his hair and his face. One eye didn't go exactly straight. I'd seen Sgt. Tucker chew out three Rangers at the same time and not one of the students knew who he was chewing out, but they thought it must have been them because his eye went crazy to the side.

They grafted hair from somewhere else on his body and put it on his head, but it wasn't regular hair. It never combed quite right; it always wanted to curl up and go the other way. His nose was sort of burned and you could see up in his head a little bit there. I had some questions for this sergeant assigned to the barracks

"Are you a ranger instructor?," I asked, since he had a subdued, almost dark camouflage Ranger tab, rather than black and gold.

"Yea, I'm a ranger instructor. What's wrong with you?"

"I was just wondering," I replied. "If you're going to be in this barracks, you have to be in charge because you outrank me."

"I'm not being in charge of barracks!" he crowed. "I'm not being in charge of anything. You're in charge of the barracks and I'm sleeping in the little carrier room at the end of the barracks."

He walked off to grab a bunk and threw his stuff on it.

"I'll sleep out here. You ain't putting me in charge of nothing. I know what I'm doing."

This man was absolutely different than any soldier I'd ever met before. From that day on for three years as a Ranger instructor I never had a dull moment. This sergeant was always doing something. What would upset me so bad was that he would pass the pro-pay test every year. They would give you a test of the things pertaining to your job in the Army and if you passed and made the top 30% you would get $150 extra for pro-pay. I never passed the pro pay test in my life. Sgt. Tucker passed it every time. He was smart, but some people didn't know about Sgt. Tucker.

He only had one lung and he'd still run those Rangers 4-5 miles and come back throwing up blood. He told me if I ever told anybody he would sabotage me. I just wondered why he wanted to put himself through that. He ended up being a Ranger instructor three or four tours after that. We were running buddies. Sgt. Tucker would call me his 9 pound bouncing baby boy and we'd often go to town together. He would get us in some kind of trouble almost every time.

Sgt. Tucker once flipped his car over on Fortson Road while driving. I was over at the Clearview when some kids came in to tell me.

"Your buddy's up there with his car turned over on Fortson Road and he's out there in the ditch eating grass."

"The police there yet?" I asked.

"Yea, they just got there."

My driver's license had been suspended for three years, but I was with this woman and I was driving her car. We got up there and saw other cars parked this way and that and all over the place. I walked up and saw a policeman there with Tucker's car upside down and him lying on the ground, eating grass.

"Why are you eating grass?" I asked him.

"I'm trying to kill the alcohol on my breath. That's the only thing I got to eat where the police won't know I've been drunk."

The police approached me about my friend.

"Do you know this guy?"

"Yes. That's my buddy."

"Will you get him out of here. He's crazy!"

I got Tucker to leave and we headed back to the car. The woman sat in the middle while I drove and Tucker was hanging his arm out the passenger side window. There were so many cars around, it was hard for me to try to back out to leave. The police came down and were shining a light, motioning for me to back up. They wanted to get Knuckles out of there as bad as I did. Tucker was still having fun. He started laughing and talking to the officers.

"Look at him! The Tuck knows!" he said, referring to me. "The police backing this fool up and he hadn't had a drivers license for three years!"

"Get this fool out of here!" the police ordered, shining a light my way.

We took off from that incident, but that's the kind of thing Tucker did all the time -- and he'd get by with it. The colonel loved him. Everybody liked him, but we would definitely do some crazy stuff. We got arrested quite a few time and got into some pretty good scraps. One low point came just after graduating Ranger school.

I knew a guy who was delinquent on his payments for about two to three months on his Chevrolet Biscayne car. It was about to be repossessed, thought I didn't know it at the time, and he offered to sign the title over if I took on the payments. Not being very smart and not being familiar with such dealings, I quickly agreed. It was nearly brand new and was "something else." Here I was, Airborne, Ranger and Ranger instructor, now with a brand new car.

I went to town on payday night and I didn't bother with putting on civilian clothes. I had on my fatigue britches and T-shirt that said Sgt. Bragg on my chest, along with regular Army boots. I was riding from bar to bar down Victory Drive, pretending like I had good sense. They had a drive-in called the Streamliner Diner where they had car hops. You could also go into the diner, sit down at the bar and eat. I think they sold beer and whiskey.

It was approaching 4 a.m. when even Sgt. Tucker gave up on me and said he was leaving me, going back with some others guys there from the 44th Ranger company.

"This new car done went to your head," he told me. "You ain't acting right."

This being payday, it was still wide open. I started trying to talk to two girls in a car there. When they left the Streamliner, I went out behind them. I wasn't drunk, but I wasn't sober either. I was pretty well in between somewhere. I was riding beside them on Victory Drive, a four-lane highway with bars and car lots and everything between Columbus and Ft. Benning. I was hollering at those girls and driving beside them -- until I ran into the back of another vehicle, knocked him spinning around in a circle.

The impact pushed my car's bumper back on the wheel, but as long as I went straight I could go, but if I tried to turn left, the bumper would rub against the tire and you could smell the rubber burning. If I turned right, I could go as fast as I wanted to. Problem was, when I hit this fellow, the police were on the other side of Victory Drive coming my direction and saw it all as I tried leaving.

An officer immediately got behind me after the hit and run. He soon pulled me over because I couldn't go fast because I had to turn the wrong way a few times and that bumper rubbed my tire. One policeman went to the right side of the car and the other come over and opened my car door with his left hand and reached in and got me under my left arm, trying to pull me out. Well, I just turned around and hit him, knocking him back out into the road with my right hand. The other policeman came running around the car with his stick out.

"Look a-here now, we can talk," I offered.

This officer didn't want to talk.

He started beating me with that stick and the other policeman got up. I was doing pretty good with these two guys, but then two MPs pulled up. They jumped out and got their little sticks out. Next thing you know, I was in the middle of Victory Drive and had traffic held up both ways. People were out hollering, telling me what to do to the police as the paddy wagon came up, because most of them were soldiers down there on payday night.

I knew if I fell down they were going to start kicking me, so I just put my hands up in the air. They were all around and hit me a few more times in the legs, arms and back, as well as poking me in the stomach with the end of the stick. They threw me on the ground and handcuffed me.

They asked if they could move my car. I told them no. Then they threatened to tow it.

"Oh, well you can move my car," I replied, just before they threw me in the paddy wagon.

When I got to jail, they put me in a cage with all the drunks who had regurgitated in that area. There was just a hole drain in the middle in this place with nothing but bars all around. I found a place that was rather clean, but wet, because everything in there was wet because they washed it down with a hose. There were four or five guys in there just laying around passed out. I probably went to sleep.

My T-shirt was torn and bloody. My fatigues looked terrible. I had contusions on my head, a broken nose, one eye swollen shut and my mouth busted all up. There were whelps on my arms and under my legs you could see where they hit me with those billy sticks. Jailers woke me up and told me to come on. They didn't let me wash my face.

I was taken down the hall and placed in a room with five or six prostitutes.

"Somebody beat you to death. You look terrible," one of them said.

The blood had dried on my face, head, shirt and arms. It was about 9 or 10 o'clock in the morning. When they opened the other door in that room, it led into a courtroom full of people. They called the prostitutes out one at a time and the judge fined them or whatever he did to each one of them. They called my name and the bailiff told me to get on out there.

I looked pitiful walking into the courtroom in front of about 200 people. They read 12 counts against me: resisting arrest, striking a policeman, striking a policeman with malice, hit-and-run, no license, no tags -- I don't recall all the charges they had against me. The judge asked how I pleaded. I said, "I don't know."

"I can tell you one thing, you were there," he said, looking at my sad condition. "I can see you were there."

The judge bound me over to the county because the hit-and-run started in the county and ended in the city. They took me to the county stockade. I was given striped clothes and told to take a shower. There were about 20 guys in the stockade building, where you could walk outside to a grass area.

It was just around noon. I couldn't eat anything because my mouth was swollen. I was trying to drink water. I went out and there was a little guard house with a man in it by the gate. I told him I hadn't had a phone call and I would like to call my momma.

"You in the Army ain't ya? And you've done hit a police officer and broken his jaw?" he replied in a gruff tone. "You don't get to call anybody. You're going to go to jail for a while, son."

I begged again to call my momma in Nankipooh.

"You're from Nankipooh?" he said.

"Yea, I went to Nankipooh school until the seventh grade."

"I didn't know you were from right here in Muskogee County," he said as his tone changed. He let me make that call.

I told momma where I was and that it was my fault for cutting up, though they beat me pretty badly. She said she was coming down there with some of her friends. Momma pulled up with three other women: Ethel Lett and two other women from Nankipooh. When they saw me, they went to the fence crying and carrying on something awful.

"Oh my Lord, they done beat this poor boy up. He ain't never done nothing and he wasn't right in the head. He couldn't read and they just took advantage of him!"

"Oh my Lord have mercy, who could have done something to such a pitiful boy and he always had a good heart."

Momma went in the guard house and got some people on the phone, followed by some bad language out her mouth. It wasn't any time before they told me I was being released in the care of my momma. She told them this wasn't the end of the matter and there was no reason anybody should beat anybody in such a way. They tried explaining I had resisted arrest and fought back.

"I don't care!" she interrupted. "Y'all shouldn't have done this to him."

I went back to Nankipooh that night with momma. Sunday afternoon she carried me back to Ft. Benning. I went over to the committee building Monday morning to meet Master Sgt. Joe Cason, who told me to see Maj. Gouch in charge of the Ranger instructors.

I was told my conduct was unbecoming of an NCO and it was no way for a man in the Army to act, especially when it could give them a bad reputation. I could only say I didn't mean to get into trouble. Maj. Gouch told me to get back to the barracks and take it easy because I didn't look good. As I walked away, there was some majors and captains and other ranger instructors around.

"Now there goes a real Ranger. He's tough," I heard one of the officers say.

I got around to checking on my car and found out I still had to pay for it. Turns out, they'd already auctioned the car off for little or nothing and told me I had to pay a big bill for the balance of the car. Well, we agreed on me giving them a dollar a month and requested a receipt. See, in the Army, every unit got what they call an "s---house lawyer." These guys will tell you all your legal stuff. This one sergeant that was an shithouse lawyer is the one who told me all I had to do was to pay a dollar a month, but to make sure I had a receipt, even send a money order for proof, and they couldn't do anything to me. If I missed one month, however, I had to come up with the rest of the money. I paid it for that three years and then when I went to Okinawa, I sent them money from over there every month.

After I came back from Okinawa, I didn't send them any more money and I didn't hear anything else from them because they auctioned that car off to one of the operator's relatives for about half what it cost. The only thing wrong with it was the bumper bent back on the tire. That's the way they did soldiers, though. If they caught a soldier, there was a line of people right down the highway off base waiting to take advantage. It's the same thing overseas. They have a regular price for regular folks, but when a soldier comes in, they have to stick it to him because he's from somewhere else, plus he doesn't have time to bargain.

You may have noticed a theme of how I was good as any soldier when I was in the field, especially as a Ranger instructor, but bad things happened when I went to town. I wasn't smart enough and didn't have the social skills to be in those situations, but it didn't stop me from going.

On Sundays, they only sold alcohol on the base. Across from Ranger department about a mile or so was Victory Lodge. On Sundays Victory Lodge was packed, even though it was way out in the woods.

People would come from everywhere. It was a big place overlooking the lake and you could get alcohol to drink. Sgt. Tucker and I were over at Victory Lodge one night, minding our own business like we're supposed to. In through the door came about 15 guys with one big ol' boy. They walked through Victory Lodge all the way out back to the screen porch and started pushing people around, making them move and pushing tables together to make themselves one big table. I later found out ol' big boy was a weightlifter. Back then not many people lifted weights. His nickname was Superman. He was about 6'4" and weighed about 250 pounds, wearing a T-shirt over his rippled stomach.

Superman went to a table and told this married woman he wanted to dance. Her husband told him she didn't want to dance. Superman just dragged the woman up and was dragging her around the dance floor. Her husband went and told the bouncer and the bouncer asked me what I was going to do about this wild bunch.

"You're the bouncer. You get paid to fight crazy people, not me."

No more than when I said that, someone pointed out Tucker in the latrine getting into a fight with some of those guys. I walked over and saw Tuck arguing with two of Superman's buddies. The big fella ran the main post gym and was a bodybuilder. I tried to settle the matter with both sides. They called us dumb rebels.

"You're crazy. The Civil War has been over!" I said.

Superman stormed up wanting to know what was going on. His buddies said this ugly one (Tucker) started telling them what they can and can't do and he's just a silly rebel.

"Tuck's from Ohio!" I explained. "He ain't from the south."

"He sure looks like a dumb rebel to me."

I tried another attempt at civility.

"We're all in the same Army. If we said anything or did anything, I apologize."

The big bodybuilder with his ripples in his stomach only pushed harder.

"You"re a yellow-bellied rebel and a coward."

"Well, I might be," I replied, seeing where this was going. "I ain't no Indian, but I know war talk when I hear it. We might want to step outside, I reckon."

Everyone piled outside Victory Lodge to watch us go at it. He cussed me and called me everything in the world. I kept telling him the Civil War is over and wondering what is wrong with him. He persisted to call my relatives names also, including my mother and father. He was so big and muscular. I was a little scared of him, to tell you the whole truth. By this time, this little sergeant who'd been in there came out asking who was talking about a rebel.

He ran up to Superman, who immediately pushed him down. When he did, I swept Superman's legs out from under him and he hit the ground. I don't think anyone really knew who knocked Superman down or if he fell down. He got up and looked around at everybody except me. I don't think he knew what happened. He told his guys he was ready to go. They got their cars and left the parking lot.

But it wasn't over yet. After we got back to the lodge, people were coming by to egg me on.

"I never thought I'd ever hear someone talk to you that way and you'd take it," one said.

"Did you see how big he was? His arms and muscles? That's a big boy!"

"Yea, but we didn't think a Ranger would let anybody talk to him and call him names like that."

"I wasn't going to let him go on too much longer I don't think."

Naturally, my reputation as a number one hand-to-hand instructor and a bad man fell pretty quickly, even though I didn't get a whooping, just a cussing. I got angrier the more I thought about it all week. Every time I turned around at Ranger department, somebody would come up and say they heard I got cussed out and didn't do anything about it even when he called my momma names.

Now, I know that would be the proper thing to do. Back then, for young men, there was no way you were supposed to let someone talk to you in such a manner.

That next weekend, I went up to Mike Salazar's house. He made corn whiskey. I drank a bit of corn whiskey that Sunday morning and drove back to Ranger department, got some food, laid down in my bunk and waited until 7 p.m. I put on my glad rags and went to Victory Lodge. I made up my mind there wasn't going to be any talking this time. There wasn't going to be nothing but dust flying, because I was not going to let anyone ruin my reputation and make everybody think I was a coward.

I sat there drinking beer until about 9 p.m. I thought they weren't going to come around this late. Tucker was walking around talking about his 9 pound bouncing baby boy is mad.

"You can tell he's mad. Look at him! He's been upset all week," he went on. "My 9 pound bouncing baby boy is ready. I knew he's ready. If them boys come out here, there's going to be a bunch of them toting a whooping." (Toting a whooping is South Georgia talk.)

I, on the other hand, was trying to act normal, but I have to admit I had been really worried and mad and disgusted with myself over the whole thing. Finally, I saw them coming. About 15 of them barged through the middle of the club out to the porch making people move, sliding tables together, with Superman leading the pack. I sat there a while, but they weren't doing anything but talking. I thought this ordeal is crazy and really dumb. I went back there to settle things reasonably.

"Look, if I said or did anything last week I apologize. I got no gripe with you guys, whether you're from the north, south, east or west."

After I apologized, everyone at the table said I was right. One or two got up and shook my hand. Then I put my hand out to Superman.

"I don't shake hands with no yellow-bellied rebel and coward," he sneered.

That was all I could take.

"You better get outside. Outside, right now!"

I ran outside waiting for him. He came out cussing and calling me names. I jumped up and hit him in the chest with both hands, pushed him back. I pushed him back again and again toward the parking lot.

"Why don't you fight?" I said. "yYou got all your friends out here with you."

The only person I had was Tucker and he couldn't fight -- but he could start the fight. Superman had all his buddies with him. I asked him to come down to the hand-to-hand pit at the bottom of the hill if he thought I had all kinds of friends around for backup. I ran down the hill where we put on our Ranger demonstration at the hand-to-hand pit and bleachers. He finally came walking down there.

I kept trying to talk sense to him, saying this whole thing was crazy. He kept on calling me a coward, so, I hit him. The blow knocked him down and I jumped on top of him and started beating him in the dark in a culvert ditch. I got up and his mouth and nose were bloodied. He was swollen and had blood running down his face. I didn't have a scratch on me. All I did was break my right hand. (I hit the ground instead of him one time.)

"You're so hard-headed," I told him.

"You're a yellow-bellied rebel," he replied defiantely.

"You can't fight! You're big and strong, but you can't fight!" I said, before returning to the top of the hill. Folks asked if Superman was all right.

"He's too hard-headed and crazy. You can't hurt him. He'll be all right."

Superman wandered up the hill and went straight to his car and left. I went back to the club, drank a beer and went to the hospital. I got a cast put on my hand and went back to Ranger department. The next day I was asked what happened. Sgt. Hawthorne had this account: "Ranger Bragg went out there, growled and hit a Ranger sign and broke his hand." That's the kind of stuff that happened at Ranger department. Your friends always have something nice to say about you. Later in Vietnam, a Sgt. Hawthorne left a hospital against doctor's orders. The aircraft carrying him was shot down on the way back to his unit. A lot of Rangers got killed returning to the fight when they didn't have to.

I raised sand with some Ranger students in my first three years at Ranger department, but I also grew up a lot. I earned a reputation that people still talk about today. I had no intention of doing anything other than keeping a job, but I got in more trouble than you can believe. I did not get busted at Ranger department, but I still had the reputation.

I eventually received orders around 1963 to report to Okinawa. I was assigned to the 503rd Charlie Company and was a rifle squad leader. I had little trouble, but I was picked to train in self-defense and counter-insurgency operations because I was a Ranger. We had people volunteering to go to Vietnam around that time, but you had to join the Special Forces, where they would send you for 6 months as advisors to the South Vietnamese army. Most of my buddies did and they tried to get me to do it. For some reason, I didn't want to do that.

Someone once told me if I wanted to move up in the Army, I needed to get some college education. I only had an 8th grade education, but they said anyone could go to this English 101 class taught at Okinawa. I decided to go and get at least one college class. We got down to the classroom, which already had too many people there. The instructor decided to thin the herd a bit.

He went around the classroom and asked everybody a question. The first time he came around he asked a fellow to define nouns and pronouns. He asked what was a conjunction. I told him that's where two roads cross. The instructor came back to ask four of us a second question. He asked me to explain what you would be looking for in a vertical file in the library. I said that was one of those files that goes straight up and down. He asked me to step out of the classroom with two or three other guys. I thought he wanted me to be an assistant instructor or help him because I got two questions right. Instead, he told us we needed remedial training. I didn't know what remedial training was. I didn't know if he was promoting us beyond that class, but finally he told me I had to take classes to get into that class. I wasn't smart enough for it.

While in Okinawa I set up repelling and mountaineering training for the whole 173rd down on an island called Iriomote and another island nearby was called Ishigaki. Each year I spent about three months down there training in escape and evasion, patrolling, survival, but mainly repelling and mountain climbing. One fine day I was ordered to report to Ft. Buckner, which is near Sukaran. Ft. Buckner was headquarters for all Army operations in Asia.

When I arrived a major told me he wanted me to pick any 10 men in the 173rd I wanted. It was for a secret mission involving smugglers taking contraband to an unsettled island. We would be tasked with discretely capturing these civilians.

As we got organized I thought for him, in all of Southeast Asia, to pick me, a young E-5 sergeant, to run a patrol against some civilians with live ammunition was unique. We were told we probably would have contact because these people were heavily armed and were trained in stealing some expensive stuff and using that island as a weigh station. And we definitely couldn't talk about it.

We sneaked onto that island, somewhere between Okinawa and Japan. They had a tunnel where they stored stolen goods. They also had a huge yacht that was absolutely beautiful, which they used to haul stuff. They had drugs, stolen property and equipment -- just about anything. We caught them with such surprise, we were able to accomplish the mission without much of a skirmish. The Army brought in other people immediately and had us load up to go back to Okinawa.

They told us we didn't see anything or know anything. Higher command personnel got credit for doing it and we were never mentioned. We never even got a letter. I thought to myself, we must be pretty special to get an assignment like that, but I thought about it after the years went and realized that if we'd been killed, they could have passed it off that we were just some ol' country boys who died in a training exercise. Sometimes you think you're a hero, when you're really just a poor guinea pig. And on most missions it's hard to decide which way that goes.

Aside from my duties leading training and the special mission, we were instructed to run a combat simulation in Southeast Asia with all the units in Okinawa, Japan, Korea and Hawaii. We, the whole 173rd, went to Clark Air Base and marshal. In other words, we lived on Clark Air Base out on the air field. Our "home" for about three weeks was where the plane took off and landed, with the heat and the bugs, living out of our rucksacks. We probably got one hot meal a day. Other than that, we're just out in the sun, baking.

I was a jumpmaster on what I think was a C124. This aircraft had 120 paratroopers, inboard and outboard. That means you had a row of paratroopers sitting with their backs to each other down the center of the aircraft, or inboard personnel, while another stick or paratrooper faced them with their backs to the outside of the aircraft, or the outboard. There was also an upstairs with inboard and outboard personnel. The jumpmaster is in charge of all troopers on that aircraft.

In the front of the plane, you had two spiral staircases. When you gave jump commands, these people on the upstairs had to start coming down to get in line to jump out the back of the airplane. There was a door on both sides of the aircraft.

After marshaling for three weeks at Clark Air Base and living like animals out of a rucksack, we loaded up to fly from Clark Air Base to Korat, Thailand. Korat is in the central highlands of Thailand, north of Bangkok about 50-75 miles. We put our parachutes on, checked out all of the men, loaded them on the aircraft and took off. This was about an 8 to 12-hour flight over Vietnam and Laos.

We'd been flying about 10 hours, very uncomfortable with your parachute pack pulling your shoulders down. There was a Cpl. Pruitt who I had put through Ranger school before I went to Okinawa. He would always get busted from sergeant to corporal, but many times he was in charge of people who had two or three more stripes than he did. Pruitt was a great soldier, a Ranger.

Cpl. Pruitt was about the fifth or sixth man on the outboard stick as we were flying. I saw him get a burp bag (a little paper bag in the aircraft) and pour water from his canteen into the burp bag. Then he just sat it down between his legs and put the canteen up. I wondered what he was up to, because from where I was at in the rear of the plane I could see all the way up the four sticks. As soon as the red light came on signaling 20 minutes before the jump, Cpl. Pruitt started making like he was sick. He began acting like he was throwing up in the burp bag, making all kinds of noise to get attention and moving his head around. Then he shook his head, wiped his mouth off and yelled, "Airborne!" and turned the burp bag up and drank the water out of it. About 10 guys regurgitated all over themselves and others at the same time after seeing that. I said to myself, when I get that boy on the ground I'm gonna kill him.

Cpl. Pruitt was one of those characters you find in the Army that you really don't want to have around unless he's in charge. If he's in charge, he runs everything pretty well. If he's not, he can cause you a few problems.

In this simulated combat jump, we had full equipment, rations, machine guns, ammunition and everything. The first 15-20 guys on the aircraft would jump out with a PAE bag -- a four-foot high, two-foot wide square holding all the equipment we needed to fight a war. Being a jumpmaster, I had to check out all these guys and make sure they had the PAE bag hooked on the front parachute with the D-rings and then give the jump commands. Jump commands are 'Get Ready," "Stand up," "Hook up," and "Check your equipment," which means especially checking the static line hooked to the cable running through the top of the aircraft and down to the back of the parachute, since it will eventually pull your chute out.

After they were standing and sounding of for equipment check, the next command given was "Stand at the Door." They would jump out both sides and rear of the aircraft when the green light came on. Just before that, however, a fellow in the back accidentally pulled his reserve parachute while coming down the steps. This happens as we have quite a number of other aircraft in formation for the mass tactical combat jump.

They hollered for me to help, over all the noise from the plane doors being open. I unhooked my static line, connected it to my main left well. I grabbed a reserve and crawled over, through, under to get to the front of the plane. Took off his chute and rucksack, put on his new reserve, then put everything back together. By the time I got him ready, the green light was on and the plane was empty. The only ones left on board were the loadmaster, this paratrooper and me. I checked the trooper one last time before he ran and jumped out the airplane. I hustled down to the door to jump -- and I froze.

I hadn't hooked back up. I detached my static line from the main left well and hooked back on the jump cable. I finally lept out the plane and started looking for the other paratroopers. Way down there about 15-20 miles from me, I saw the last troopers going down behind the trees. I looked at the ground with the jungle and the terrain to see if there were any trails or roads going that way. It was nothing but mass jungle below me.

My jump ended with me landing in a tree in the middle of the jungle in northern Thailand: a jungle stretching all the way to China, Vietnam, Burma and west India. You don't want to get lost in a jungle that big.

I finally got out of the tree and loaded up my parachute, rucksack, reserve, weapon and harness and started walking in the direction I thought the Drop Zone was in. All I could think about was that I am a long way from the DZ with night coming. Dark rolled in, but I found a small trail to follow. I eventually came upon some hooches where a little bitty dog was barking. The trail went right through the hooches. So much for stealth.

"Oh my Lord," I remember thinking. "I don't know who these people are and they don't know who I am."

The hooches were made with bamboo walls, a primitive thatch roof over dirt floors. I saw an old man pull a cloth curtain back from the hooch door and he had a paralyzed gaze when he saw me. I can just imagine this man seeing some stranger at night in the early 1960s walking through his village with all this equipment.

I walked until I gave out and went to sleep on the ground. I got up the next day and started walking again. The trail turned into a little road and I went through a few more villages, By noon the following day I arrived at the DZ, only to find most everyone was gone. I turned in my parachute and got ready to move on. Fortunately, as a squad leader, I knew our mission and which direction to go from our planning and caught up to our platoon the next day at noon. I was glad that entire episode ended uneventfully.

After the jump and running our mission, we were brought back to a field with few bushes and no trees for about 3,000 paratroopers to camp. We were told we'd be there for a week or so as our group went back to Okinawa a few flights at a time. The field has a bad case of snakes and scorpions, so we were told to build a bed up off the ground but there weren't any sticks or limbs. We ended up sprawled out in grass and weeds, worrying about waking up with scorpions and snakes all over us.

Around the second night or so, they let half the outfit go to town. I didn't want to go to town, because I figured I might get into trouble. Instead, I went with some of the other guys to a place where they were selling beer, where we stayed for an hour or two. About 3 a.m., a private came down and told me I had to report to the consolidated mess hall, an old building where they had been feeding us.

When I got up there, two or three company commanders were there, two or three first sergeants from other companies were there with my company commander and my first sergeant. They told me I'd been caught and they knew I was one of the ones who went downtown. They demanded I tell them my part in an "incident" that happened hours earlier. I told them I didn't know what happened because I wasn't there. They said two guys in my squad informed them the "big white guy that talks like a black person" got away."

"And that's you," they scolded me.

Over the next couple of hours, I kept telling them they had me mistaken for someone else. They had questioned me and took me from one company commander to another, then to the MPs and provost marshal and provost sergeant, taking turns and interrogating me that night. I didn't even know what happened until the next day when somebody else told me. efore that, they were hoping I would tell them things they didn't know. All that was going on as my first sergeant was trying to blame it on me.

I later learned that 13 soldiers had gone to town and turned over a two-story bus, killing some Thailanese people, maybe four or five. Other American soldiers, non-paratoopers -- we called them Legs -- tried to stop them. The group of soldiers beat those two Legs near to death, then attacked the provost marshal and the provost marshal's sergeant, turning over their jeep. They escaped the mob and the provost marshal got as many of his MPs and other guys together. This group of about 30 to 40 men went down the dirt road leading to where we stayed and got on both sides of the road for an ambush. When those 13 guys came down the dirt road to get back down to the field, still acting rowdy and drinking, the MPs encircled and caught all of them except the ringleader.

And some were saying I was the ringleader who got away.

I had been taken to the hospital to stand before one of the American soldiers they beat so badly. They took me into his room, already knowing who the other 12 guys were, but I guess he told them it wasn't me.

A magazine article later labeled the international incident as "The 13 Ugly Americans." They put me in charge of those 12 guys in a barracks building for a few days, but only until this major from Washington, D.C. brought his staff to Thailand to interrogate us about incident details. I would march these guys down to the chow hall and march them back each meal. I also had to march them down at 8 a.m. for a week to a place where they interviewed us one by one. At least three days passed before this major from Washington interviewed me. Things actually looked favorable for me at this point.

"You know, I'm pretty satisfied in my mind that you weren't one of them," he told me. "All of these guys are saying you are not the one, but they won't tell us who it was that got away."

The "13 Ugly Americans" matter was a dangerous situation. It's a wonder I didn't go to jail. These soldiers were eventually sent to Leavenworth, Kansas to do time -- 5, 10, 20 years -- I don't know how much. As far as I know, they never did find out who was the ring-leader, because those boys wouldn't tell even after they went to jail for senseless killings.

Why would any humans do that? When you're in the Army or other branch and you go to another country, you're away from home. Some believe your friends won't ever find out what you do. They don't really think and they do some crazy, stupid things. If I had been there, I would have fought them to make sure that didn't happen. I would never participate in something like that against my soldiers or residents of another country. Sometimes soldiers or any group of men can get a mob mentality.

After the major released me, I went down and requested my flight back to my unit in Okinawa. By this time all of the 173rd was gone. All the other troops from Hawaii and Korea were gone and there were only a few aircraft left.

I was told of a flight leaving out there soon, but it has equipment on it. That didn't matter to me, so I sat in a jeep inside the aircraft to fly out of Thailand. I didn't go back to my unit when I returned to Okinawa. I went to a Capt. Kirby Smith that I knew from Ranger department and told him he had to get me out of that unit, that company, because the company commander and the first sergeant were out to get me. They were the ones who falsely accused me of those atrocities in Thailand. Smith made good on my request.

"You go get your gear out of that Charlie company and come down here. You're in Troop E, 17 Cav. now -- in my company," Smith said.

We worked together in the northern training area of Okinawa, which is a beautiful island with peaceful people. A few months later I was set to return to the States. Then came a cruel twist as I was boarding a plane to leave Kadena Air Base in Okinawa.

The Army called an alert to send the 173rd to Vietnam. It was my men -- but not me.

I didn't know it at the time. The call came as I got on the plane going back to the States and I had probably missed it by mere minutes, but no more than an hour. Capt. Smith had tried to call and get me pulled from my flight before it left, but it was too late. It wasn't until I was on the road in California in a brand new car that I heard via radio the 173rd had deployed to Vietnam. If I had known they were on alert, I would not have gotten on that plane. I would have sent my family back to America, but I would have gone to Vietnam with my unit, the 173rd.

It's a strange feeling when you trained a group of men -- and I had trained everyone in the 173rd in something in the three years as an instructor -- to know now they were over there facing the enemy and here I am in the States. You know some of those guys are going to die and the training I gave them could have an effect on whether they lived or died in some cases.

It didn't feel quite right, but I had a new assignment when I returned stateside. I was sent back to Ranger department to get others ready for battle in Vietnam. We started running 2 and 3 ranger classes together at a time. We'd previously run about 10 classes through in a year. Now we had one class in training at Ft. Benning and another class coming from Florida through mountain Ranger camp and another class coming up about to graduate. There were 600 to 700 Rangers at a time going every whichaway as part of 15-20 classes a year. Demand for small unit leadership was high during

Vietnam.

I went back to doing hand-to-hand where I was the number one hand-to-hand instructor as before. I fell right back into it, demonstrating bayonet, pugil sticks, demolitions and basic patrolling. I was also assigned as an assistant principal instructor for Camp Darby, which I had helped locate when I was in my first tour.

This was also a time when soldiers didn't make any money. We could have qualified for food stamps and welfare easily, especially for an E-5 and below. I was an E-6. When I took work details out to Camp Darby, I would drive along the roads slowly and pick up soda bottles to cash in to pay for breakfast or dinner. Breakfast was about 22 cents at the Army mess hall and a soda bottle was worth around three cents. Some other bottles were a nickel, but even then it took several to cover my meals each day.

I really made my money throwing bayonets and hatchets out at Camp Darby. I'd have work details build bunkers, dig holes and set up all these objectives for the Ranger students for when they patrolled recon objectives where the aggressors set up. Typically, I'd bet one man on these details that I could throw a bayonet and stick it. Then I'd continue to bet them from a big tree down to a four-inch tree. I could throw it where it would spin one time over an 8 to 10 foot span. Then the stakes raised to 15 foot making it spin two turns before it stuck. I would throw it very hard so when it hit it stuck. I did the same thing with the hatchet. I would bet a quarter that I could throw the hatchet so well and stick it in a 2x4. I did pretty good with betting on my knife and hatchet throwing.

Along with picking up soda bottles, I've always had a basic instinct for making money somehow -- but I always made nickels, dimes or quarters. I'd arm-wrestle people, too. I'd pull most any kind they want to do. Mercy was something I used to do with guys for money. That's where you put your hands in the air and interlock fingers, then push each other down and try to get the advantage by twisting the wrist. I did that to quite a few people and made them say "mercy" because I always worked hard and my hands are strong.

And work I did while handling two jobs.

I had to go to Camp Darby and put details to work, then come back and demonstrate hand-to-hand and bayonet. The man who took over API Camp Darby only ran it as assistant instructor to build bunkers, classrooms and all of the bleachers and related structures, but I had to do both jobs. I was told the reason they kept me on so many details and jobs everyday was to keep me out of trouble because I had so much energy.

Ranger school had nearly doubled its instructors to around 40 and included a colonel, majors, captains and master sergeants. Since we had so many Ranger instructors, the colonel planned a party at his house with mandatory attendance for everyone. I didn't want to go, but Sgt. Cogburn told me I had to be there. He also told me, however, I could go in and have one glass of beer or tea and eat a cookie or two and leave.

"Don't say much to anyone and you won't get into trouble," he said.

The colonel lived in the officer quarters down main post at Ft. Benning. When I arrived, his wife opened the door and reached around to hug me. Lord have mercy I had already been in so much trouble with women I wasn't about to get into any more. I set my hands on both her shoulders and pushed her back. She started cutting up a bit, which brought the colonel out to ask what was the matter.

"Sgt. Bragg pushed me! He hit me and knocked me back."

"What's wrong with you?" the colonel said to me.

"Well she tried to hug me. I can't be hugging your wife."

"I think you better leave, Sgt. Bragg."

I hurried away before I got in any more trouble. That may sound like a stupid move, but even though I'd been in the Army a while, I still had never had any social activity to refine my interaction with people. I didn't know when you went to people's houses that they hug one another. In Nankipooh, if a man had come up there hugging another man's wife there would have been a shooting – or killing.

Not long after, the colonel planned another party at a hunting lodge, somewhere in the woods near Sand Hill. We had a lot of officers and enlisted people, so we might have had 35-40 men there with their wives, along with a band playing. This building was sort of open and didn't have a ceiling, so you could see up through the trusses. I finally got restless after consuming a little bit of beer and started looking for something to do.

"Look here, I can do pull-ups on these trusses," I boasted.

Being tall, I reached them and I was going down through the building hand after hand on the trusses down to one end and come back showing off how strong I was. Everybody was laughing and carrying on. You could see the electric wires and light bulbs with a string where you turn them on and off. It was sort of a primitive building, but it was big enough for my showcase while guests drank and ate.

Some of them had some I , young, good-looking women. I saw the colonel dancing with one of the lieutenant's wives when he slid his hand down her behind.

"Ain't this here something? The colonel out there doing such a thing," I thought.

So I told the colonel's wife about her husband's inappropriate act.

"He's supposed to be an officer and a gentleman," I said. "He's not supposed to be doing anything like that."

She started crying. The colonel showed up and asked what was wrong. I told him exactly what I told his wife. They left the party soon after that.

I wonder why I never got promoted and always had trouble. That colonel hated me after telling on him. My name was on the board assigned to detail day and night. Many said I could do anything in Ranger department better than most anybody else after two years, but I would always speak my mind.

I was getting ready to leave one day when I saw the promotion board with a bunch of E-6's there. I had more time and grade as an E-6 than anybody and I'd been a Ranger instructor longer than any of them. I had to go get a detail that Saturday morning when they had the promotion board on the main post at Ft. Benning, then go to Harmony Church about 20-30 miles away to get detail crews there and take them another 20 miles to Camp Darby for work. My day continued by going back change into my Class A clothes, heading to main post another 10 miles to get in line as the last one to go before the board. As soon as the board session ended, I was back at Ranger department, upstairs to the lounge to take off my khakis and put on fatigues.

I hustled downstairs and found nobody else was there. There was no class there, just the colonel in his office. I walked to the work board right outside his office and looked over what I had to do. (Most of the guys are off when there wasn't Ranger class in, but not me.) I overheard the colonel talking.

"Well everybody passed the E-6 board then. Promote all of them -- except Sgt. Bragg. I don't think he's ready yet."

I hadn't always acted with sense and this moment wasn't going to be any different when I heard what he was doing to me. I barged into his office started screaming at him about how I could do any-thing out there and I could do things he couldn't do. Run five miles? He couldn't run five miles! And he surely couldn't do hand-to-hand combat like me in front of students. I was a ranking E-6 and he was promoting those guys beneath me? Yeah, I was mad.

There was nobody there but us and you could tell he was scared. Thankfully, I didn't touch him. I walked out and went back to Camp Darby to work my detail. It wasn't long after that I got orders to go to Vietnam, which was probably the best thing in the world for me and my career as a soldier.

The colonel got orders to Alaska. He wasn't there a long time before I heard he died in a helicopter crash.

I tried to keep it all business in this duty. For once, I wasn't getting into a lot of trouble or fights. I barely even went to town. I was no longer a young, uneducated man without guidance on how to act. I had matured and was able to teach and be a much better instructor than I was the first three years in Ranger department. Perhaps the only drawback is that my reputation stayed the same -- and that sometimes drew other "tough guys" my way.

A group of instructors from the school at Ft. Bragg, North Carolina were sent over to Raider school to help train students because we had so many coming through. When these boys came down, they had a guy named Sutton who was supposed to be the meanest fella at the Ft. Bragg school.

"People are talking about who can whoop who," some of the guys told me. "You or Sgt. Sutton: who is the baddest man out here?"

"Lord have mercy, why me?"

Despite my surprise, they told me there was talk about him wanting to fight me.

I was spending time upstairs in the game room -- you might call it a community lounge, with pool table and ping pong table and couches -- when we weren't at a class. A few regular Ranger instructors were with me when Sutton strolled in with a few of his buddies. He immediately started talking about how he thought he was the baddest man in the Ranger department and he can beat me in a fight. I didn't have time for that.

"Yea, you could whoop me," I told him. "We'll let it go that way, if that's good."

"No, we're going to fight," he declared.

"Ain't this a mess?" I said to the other instructors as I looked away from him. That's when he saw an opening and punched me in the chest.

They say if you hit someone over their chest, it will jar their heart and knock them out. When he hit me over my heart, however, he immediately grabbed his hand and held it down between his legs, screaming about how he had busted his hand. Everybody was telling me

"Jump on him. Get him! Kill him! He sucker punched you!" my backers were saying.

"Nah, if he's stupid enough to hit a Ranger, just let him suffer," I said. "There's no need hurting him any more."

I stepped out confidently and walked down the steps and went over to the barracks, because I was about to pass out. I took off my field jacket and noticed the Army compass in my vest pocket. They're about 2 inches square and a half inch to an inch deep, made out of hard plastic, like iron or metal. Sutton had hit me on that compass. While it hurt his hand, it cut me so bad I was bleeding. I got the blood stopped and laid there for 30 minutes to an hour. I finally got up, put on a jacket and went walking to the mess hall. I could hear the Ranger instructors talking when I walked in.

"I told you he was crazy. He doesn't know his strength. You can't hurt him."

The stories that get told about that incident are unbelievable. It turned into where three guys had hit me at the same time and all three broke their fists. You let a story get started and it'll grow.

Every once in a while there are a few guys who say they knew me well and were with me downtown when I knocked out 10 guys, along with all kind of stuff. The stories went on and on and got worse.

Otherwise, this time at Ranger department was fairly uneventful. I spent time demonstrating hand-to-hand combat, patrolling, bayonet and demolitions. We got to make improvised charges, using sugar and black powder with other stuff. You'd stir it and then blow things up. We tried everything. Every once in a while we'd singe our hair pretty good and blow some stuff up that we weren't supposed to be doing. I said it was a fairly uneventful time.

The truth of the whole matter is, I was always wanting excitement and I would always be the daredevil. If you dared me to climb the hill, I would go climb the hill. If you tell me to jump in front of a truck, doggone if I wouldn't jump in front of the truck. I was just always ready for a challenge. I always wanted to arm wrestle or push and shove. I never meant any harm. I just could not be normal and I didn't like to just sit around and talk. I'd rather wrestle somebody than talk to them. It's just part of my makeup, growing up in a big family and not having anything, but not knowing you didn't have anything.

I loved the challenge and I loved excitement. I didn't really worry about getting hurt, because I knew if you got hurt in the Army, they'd take you to the hospital and you still got paid. That was some of the best stuff lying in the hospital with clean sheets with people bringing your food or going down to the mess hall to eat and then get back in bed. But everywhere I went, people were always drawn to me. They always wanted to talk to me and hear about Nankipooh and hear about hogs and cows and things from when I was growing up, because I could make it funny.

These incidents and things that happened to me, they just didn't happen to other people. I don't know how I was so "lucky" to get in all these messes -- to be a good soldier, yet to get in so much trouble. It's unbelievable that I did not end up in jail, busted or another terrible situation, rather than getting by.

Three good years of being a Ranger instructor passed and with it came orders for me to deploy to Vietnam. I was upset I had missed out going with the 173rd as I left Okinawa, but this was business. And I was ready for that.

In the military, I didn't read the paper. I didn't stay up with current events and I didn't really know the politics of the war. You really can't get involved in the politics of the war, if you're a soldier. You do what you're told to do, right or wrong.

I was expecting to get orders before I did because Vietnam started when I got back to the States. Instead I went through almost three years of training Ranger students while people I served with in the 173rd were already being killed in Vietnam or on their second tour, while I had never been.

But emotions didn't get in my way as I prepared to head into combat. You train for war in the airborne and rangers and, in a sense, you're glad there is a war because that's what you are there for. Not everybody in elite units are that way, but for me that's how I felt about my first trip to Vietnam.

War is my business -- and business is good.

CHAPTER 5 -- FACE TO FACE
WITH THE VIET CONG

Never underestimate the power of motivation.

What may seem like the craziest of inspirations can help you succeed -- and keep you alive in many cases.

To be a good leader and to motivate your men, you've got to get over this thing about what's really going on during war. They need to be eager to get to business.

During Vietnam, my unit's motto was, "If you can't bleed, don't die." That's what my recon platoon said all the time as we trudged through anything the war and terrain dealt us. Some guys would say it was hot or they had dysentery or didn't feel good.

"Well if you can't bleed, don't die. Let's go!"

And that's how it went because, you know, basically war is crazy and it's that type of talk that really makes people respond.

One of my favorite stories from the second World War is of the 442nd charging German Pill boxes -- cement bunkers. When they started rushing up the hill, the Germans were just cutting them to pieces. When they got over halfway up, some guys started retreating down the hill and some hid. They were all going to be killed if they didn't go up or down the hill.

Then a private stood up and said, "Go for broke! Go for broke!"

The other guys started hollering it and everyone resumed charging. It electrified them.

"Go for broke!"

Guys running down the hill turned around.

"Go for broke!"

Those men overran the Germans. Over half the unit was killed but they ran off the Germans and killed more of them in the end.

Motivation is something you can't put a price on. If you have a group of men and you motivate them, you can accomplish any mission. But if you have a group of men and they're not motivated, they will end up doing more harm to themselves than you can ever imagine. You get a unit to believe in you and you motivate them, they know you'd be willing to die for them. You have to be willing to die for them because they're going to be willing to die for you.

When you fight in war, you don't fight for your country. You don't fight for your family. You fight for the other guy in that foxhole with you or that guy on patrol with you. You don't want to let your buddies down and you don't want to be the reason someone else gets killed.

After my first six years in the Army, I arrived in Vietnam not only a well-trained and seasoned sergeant, I was motivated, with high spirits for war and ready to accomplish any mission they assigned me. I was one of the few that would be in that frame of mind, but that's the stuff that will keep you alive. You can't halfway fight. You can't halfway do anything. If you can instill that spirit within the people around you, it's not only going to make them better, it's going to make you better.

I was addicted to winning, whether it was a fistfight or going to Ranger school. Max Haney, along with sharing the story of how I saved him from falling from that mountain cliff, also told a good example of my drive when he spoke before my induction as a Distinguished Member of the Ranger Training Brigade at a ceremony at Ft. Benning.

I had gone to lifeguard school, something that happened after some Ranger students drowned during water training in Florida.

We already had combat water survival, which was a new test put in at the Ranger department where you had to do certain things at the pool as a Ranger before you could go into Ranger school. You had to jump off in the pool with your web-gear and your weapon and go down and take your web-gear off, drop it and come back up and get out of the pool. You had to walk the 3-meter board while blindfolded. Like in the swamp in the dark and you stumble into deeper water, you have got to be able to keep your senses about you, take your web-gear off and get out of the water and save your life. So one thing you do in combat water survival, walk out on that diving board and step off in the pool.

Lifeguard class was a challenge from the beginning. The instructor told me to leave after he found out I couldn't swim. I declared to him I would graduate lifeguard school because that's what they sent me to do.

He wouldn't give in until I got a signed letter from my commander saying I was approved to stay in the class over the next two days. After that was settled, I stayed on the other end of the pool to observe. Saturday morning I joined the others on their end when the instructor gave the lifeguard test. He was still fuming at me for pushing my way into the class and watching from the other end.

"You want to be a lifeguard and you can't swim?" he said. "I'm going to jump out in the pool and you come get me."

The instructor was a great swimmer, but he yelled and flailed like he was drowning when he jumped into the pool. I followed him in and he immediately grabbed me so we both got a big mouthful of air and went down. After a while under water, he turned me loose because I wasn't fighting back. I just let him hold me. When he pushed off the bottom of the pool, I did the same and came up behind him, grabbed under his arm and put my right hand around on his throat to bring him up level to the water. I did the sidestroke and scissor kick to get him to the side of the pool whether he wanted to go or not. The instructor was turning and flipping and rolling me around, but I was still going to the side of the pool. I finally made it and heaved my water-logged instructor up over the poolside where the other boys pulled him out.

"Take him out there and give him some mouth-to-mouth. He's too damn ugly for me to kiss," I told them, in a moment that was like spiking a football after a touchdown.

Officers who were in the class with me couldn't believe I had been so hard-headed and was going to pass after completing all the requirements. No one could deny I had learned how to be a lifeguard in such a short time.

I knew my desire to accomplish a mission would help when I got to Vietnam. Before I headed out, though, I wanted to see this great country I was heading around the world to serve. I had a 30-day leave and I was going to spend that time seeing America from a Greyhound bus. I'd never traveled much except for going to Germany or anywhere with the Army, where you were in the back of a truck and you didn't get to see anything.

I got my bus ticket and departed Columbus, Georgia at dark going to Mobile, Alabama. During our nearly half-hour layover, folks told me not to walk around outside the bus station because I would get robbed. Naturally, I went outside.

"I just want someone to rob me. I'd like to see that trick."

There were a bunch of people sitting or lying on sidewalks, looking like bums. I walked around the block and came back after seeing all sorts of characters. I went back in.

"Nobody's robbed me," I pointed out.

"You were lucky."

The next leg took us to New Orleans around daylight. We were a few blocks from Bourbon Street with an hour layover, so I walked down that famous roadway about 5 a.m. There were people out there drunk. I remember people in the bars were cursing and playing loud music. I'd never seen the likes. They looked to have been acting the fool all night. I went to one bar for a beer, but the women working there were talking so nasty to people I just had to walk out of there. She was saying some things I'd never heard in my life. I mean filthy things that were unimaginable. I'd experienced enough of being around trashy folks with no morals. My best option was walking back to the bus station.

We rolled over to Waco, Texas. At the state there I saw this little fellow who was acting oddly. He might have been 30 years old or so, wearing a T-shirt and pair of khaki britches. He followed me into the station cafeteria's bathroom. He was acting weird, putting his head down in the sink, throwing water all over his head and slinging his head around, but nothing violent. I boarded the bus hoping to get away from that crazy boy. He stepped on in moments later. I think his name was Gus.

We had a super-scenic cruiser, which had the first four or five seats in front, followed by a step up four or five steps to the other seats. I sat in the rear upstairs. As we departed Waco, that fellow with the T-shirt on started having an epileptic fit. He went down the steps in the front with these older women sitting with their purses and plastic bags up against their body. Gus was cutting up and the women were hollering.

Two uniformed Marines on the bus ran over to restrain Gus, who appeared pretty strong himself. (I blended in with my civilians clothes.) The bus stopped, then I saw the driver, the Marines and Gus rolling down the steps, along the road and into a ditch.

"You look pretty big and strong," a woman told me "Why don't you go help them?"

"That boys crazy. You can see he's having a fit," I told her. "They ought to leave him alone."

I left the bus to tell them exactly that and to be careful not to let him swallow his tongue. When they let go, they saw he wasn't trying to hurt anyone. He thought he was being smothered to death, putting on a show and putting up a fight. Another bus showed up to pick up half of the women on our bus.

Gus, covered in slobber, eventually calmed down and returned to his seat. Our bus carried us onto El Paso, Texas. There was an ambulance waiting at the station. When we arrived, Gus went into another fit. He just couldn't help it. As he got off the bus, a heavy-set man in a suit ran out of the bus station and grabbed Gus. There was a plan to handle him, since someone called ahead and said they needed medical help. I told the big guy to let Gus go, but he grabbed him anyway. Gus picked up that man and laid him over the top of a car, where he fell to the ground on the other side. The two Marines finally got a hold of Gus and some guy in a long white coat, a doctor I suppose, gave Gus a shot.

We finished up a meal and rode to Albuquerque, New Mexico en route to Oakland, California. I stayed downtown that night near the bus station in a boarding house. That was a pitiful stay. It didn't cost much, but it was nasty. There were many homeless and drunk men there. It was truly sad.

A month after starting my bus journey, I had a picture of America that I'd never seen or imagined.

The next day I rode a shuttle bus to Travis Air Base where there were hundreds of soldiers processing in to go overseas as well as processing out after coming from Vietnam. All these newbies heading into Vietnam were completely different from the guys returning from Vietnam after a year. The returning veterans didn't say much.

We were eager to ask them what was going on and what we should do. All they would mostly say were things like, "Keep your head down. Don't volunteer for anything and you might make it."

Most of the men returning had dark tans and most all of them were sunburned, with cracked lips. They also had a far-away stare in their eyes. These guys were completely different, even though I was around 30 years old and these boys were around 20 years old. You could tell they had experienced something we had not. For me to notice that, being an old country boy, it had to be pretty prevalent within the troops.

We flew to Vietnam on the Freedom Bird, an airplane packed full of soldiers and amenities. There were air conditioners and clean seats along with pretty stewardesses bringing you stuff. Then we landed in Long Binh, Vietnam.

The doors opened and the heat and humidity flooded into the plane. It felt like you would just wilt before you ever exited. It was so heavy you could hardly breathe. We marched off with our duffle bags and grips. They took us to tables under a shed building lined up a long way.

"How can I stay here for a year and breathe in this heat?" I thought.

You could look down the runway and see heat coming off the runway. It was miserable. Our clothes were soaking wet with sweat within an hour. We then moved over to the RePo center (the replacement center). It was absolutely a shock even though I was from South Georgia and I knew hot days from my work logging, pulpwooding, gardening and digging holes and bomb shelters. (My mom wanted to dig a bomb shelter every year -- we knew the Russians were coming way back then. Our shelters didn't last long because she didn't know how to build a top for them. We'd put pine trees across and termites would get in there and eat them up. My brother and sister were in a bomb shelter once when it fell in and nearly killed them.)

You could tell in everybody's face we were scared. We didn't know what to expect. Being an E-6, Ranger, Airborne with a reputation as a bad man, a lot of younger men would try to befriend me. I was eventually sent to Phan Rang, Vietnam, home of the 101st base camp. There was no grass growing there because troops had stomped it down. It reminded me of back home where we had no grass because us kids wore it down with the chickens and pigs.

We were in formation when a Master Sgt. Fremmer came before us. I knew Fremmer from Ft. Benning and he like me. He was a good field soldier but he wasn't anything in garrison, getting in trouble like I did. He had been an E-5 about 18 years prior when he arrived in Vietnam. He was now already a master sergeant.

Fremmer came out of a building and kicked a canteen cup halfway across the parade field. He started chewing people out because he'd been over there nearly two years. I decided to speak with him after we broke formation.

"You know what? You've come to the right place," he told me. "You're going to love Vietnam. There's no politics over here. If you get in an argument about tactics or something, you just tell them to get their weapon and come on to the field and see if it will work."

Fremmer couldn't get promoted in peace time, though he had prospered greatly in Vietnam. It was his kind of work. He also got me in the right direction once I got there.

"You know they're starting a LRP company and they're taking volunteers right now," he told me. "This Maj. Malone, the company commander, is interviewing people right down there in that building."

I thanked him and waited until night to see Maj. Malone, who was by himself when I reported.

"Tommy Bragg! You son of a [you know what]. I'm so glad to see you," he said. "I want you to start training these people in the morning. Run then 3-5 miles and give them classes all day. We're organizing the first-ever LRP company organized in the United States Army. We will be operating with six-man teams."

Units already had LRP teams going out and being left behind, outside a perimeter of about a mile. We would be going 10-20 miles into the jungle and dropped off by helicopter. We were to be the eyes and ears of the unit we were attached to. He said he understood if I didn't want to do it.

"I wouldn't send anybody out there to do something that I wouldn't do. I'd rather be the one going to do it," I said.

The people Malone accepted would learn from me about patrolling, actions at objectives and how to read a map and call in artillery. The next morning I had about 10 guys there. We ran first and began classes after chow. Within a week, we had 40-50 guys there. We had a second platoon formed and a third platoon starting to be formed. I was talking all day and into the night with men who would ask questions. I ended up giving classes at night and I got so hoarse I could barely speak.

After about two weeks, we had the second and third platoon formed and we were sent to Camp Anari (or Dragon Mountain). We were attached to the Fourth Infantry Division for logistics, supplies, ammunition, medical care and more, yet we were under the command of the corps commander and then Maj. Malone. The corps commander was our boss and he would tell us where to go and which units we would be attached to.

And, in a sense, just like being back home, I was comfortable being in a position where soldiers needed motivation. I hate to brag, but I think I was the best around at motivating a group of guys to get something done.

Not long after arriving in Vietnam, we had to build a base camp and repelling towers. We had to put sandbags about two feet wide and four feet high all the way around the hooches and tents we made. We built everything else within a week and a half with 80 men -- half a company.

To do this, we had to fill about 20,000 sandbags. That's work you don't get a kick out of doing. One person holds a sandbag while another shovels it full of sand, then you tie the bag. Capt. Phil Mayer was in charge of the two platoons and another lieutenant there was in charge of the third platoon and two E-7s. I was an E-6 team leader. It was a Saturday and we had built the base camp. Almost everything was done and squared away ahead of schedule, which is unbelievable to do all that in a week and a half.

Capt. Mayer got us together that Saturday and said Maj. Malone would be here Monday with the fourth platoon volunteers, so we needed 20,000 sandbags by then. The guys who had been doing it didn't like doing it. The captain asked if anyone had any ideas.

"Yea. Give me two platoons after chow," I told him. "To the lieutenants and platoon sergeant: you stay at the mess hall, stay out of the way, and let me talk to these boys. I'll get all them sandbags filled, probably tonight."

I had an offer for the troops.

"If we fill these sandbags, tomorrow morning I'm going to let third platoon go down to Sin City until 12 o'clock," I told them.

Sin City was a little village not too far away. Going to Sin City for fun didn't even cost $5. When people would leave from the main gate on the road to Pleiku, prostitutes would get beside the fence. We were told not to let them go to Sin City or mingle with the prostitutes. Some of the buildings there had "laundry" on the signs, but it was a different kind of service offered when you went there. I never saw Vietnamese in a sexual way as some men did. To me, they were the enemy. I didn't hate them or dislike them, I did feel sorry for them.

I told the men if all of them came back without a problem, we were going to send the second platoon out until 4 o'clock. If anybody got in trouble or didn't come back when they were supposed to, I was personally going to whoop their behind. I wasn't joking. I was trying to motivate them, but I was going out on a limb with Capt. Mayer to let them do it.

After I dangled the prize in front of them, I followed up with a challenge. I told them my team was the best of the seven teams out there. They were so good that they didn't need me to show up the other teams.

"The rest of y'all ain't that good and my team can fill more sandbags than any other team out here. Guaranteed, no problem!" I boasted.

I told my team go ahead to start filling sandbags and they took off running. I told the second team to get ready to go.

"You think you can fill as many sandbags as my five men can do?"

"Yea, we can!"

And they took off running like a cloud of dust. I started the same conversation with the third squad, but the others squads and platoons started yelling about the others getting a head start. So, I let them all go at once. Man, at the cloud of dust and Hidy Hi-Ho Silver, people were running into each other like a bunch of cats and dogs. They were knocking each other down -- all because they wanted to fill those sandbags.

When the madness got underway, I went back to the mess hall. The lieutenant and two platoon sergeants were peeking around the barracks to see what had happened.

"Man, you had them guys running and cutting-up," one said.

"Yea, but we're going to have to let them go to town tomorrow if they do it," I reminded them. "Let's leave them alone. We don't want to let them see us."

We sat and talked over coffee for about two hours before heading out past the repelling tower and latrine to look at the field where the guys were working. You could hardly see anyone. There were 14 massive piles of sandbags filling the view. You heard the grunting as a guy held the bag as it was filled, then he would sit the sandbag to the side where another would tie it and throw it over his head. By the time he finished the toss, there was another one sitting in front of him. Each team had two groups working. That night, we essentially had enough to cover all the hooches and tents -- through motivation.

Filling sandbags was more about pride for their teams, which had just been organized a couple weeks earlier. They were more concerned about being the best team, more so than about going to town. All the soldiers came back without a problem, so we had chow afterward. We later pushed them again to finish the base camp before Monday morning.

Those you are leading have to see that you mean what you're doing. First, if men respect somebody -- and they got to have a little respect for you -- and if you portray that image of a person who will stand behind your word and not back up, they believed in you. When they believe you, it's contagious among the group. It's a similar mindset to a mob looting. That is, it's the same principle when you're motivated to do something good. The mob mentality works together to win. Forty men can destroy a town or they can build a town. They can do anything and it comes through motivation.

Our camp was ready, but there was still plenty of training to do for these young men thrust into a new world.

The second and third platoon had to build a base camp at Camp

Anari when we arrived. There were some building there, which we remodeled, such as a mess hall, barracks and some hooches. We also built a few webtops, which is a structure where you build a floor and frame, then put a tent over it. Third platoon had the mission of building the tents and filling sandbags. Second platoon, my team 2-1, was to build a latrine and the shower. (It seems like everywhere I went I got tied up with a latrine somehow. If I wasn't stealing them I was building them.)

You had to get some strong timbers like 4x4's and 6x6's because to hold up 55 gallon drums on top of the shower. In the evening, Fourth Infantry Division would bring trucks by and fill these drums with water, where you could turn on a spigot for a shower. We built the shower in about three days, with boards with cracks in them so water could run out under the bottom. It was unbelievable how my team, with one or two other guys in the unit who were carpenters, built that so quickly.

Capt. Mayer was in charge of both platoons. Our platoon sergeant was Sgt. Albright, whose nickname was Gingerbread. Lt. Mayer noted we got a lot done before Maj. Malone was to arrive with the fourth platoon. The major was still interviewing people from the 101st, mostly privates, Spec 4's and E-5's for a mission unlike the American Army had done before. The French-Indian War was probably the last time our soldiers went into the jungle to fight a fellow so adept at fighting in that terrain.

But in Vietnam, these guys fighting against us in the jungle had been born into war.

The Japanese had occupied much of Southeast Asia, China and Vietnam for years. During the second World War, we helped run Japan out of China. That's where another Ranger Unit known as Merle's Marauders were. We helped the Chinese get rid of the Japanese because the Japanese were feared all over the southeast, including Korea.

The French took hold in Vietnam because of rubber and rice resources. Vietnam had been a colony of France and the French asked for help to control the Viet Minh (North Vietnam mainly). The rice was in the delta around Saigon and the rice patties there comprised about two-thirds of all the rice in Asia because it was nearly-perfect condition for that south of Saigon. There were also huge rubber plantations in South Vietnam. We wouldn't help the French control the Viet Minh. When the French pulled out, I guess some rich people around America decided they wanted to capitalize on the rice and rubber and help the south Vietnamese break away from the north. They told us it was to stop the spreading of communism.

An old soldier who had been in Vietnam warned me about the opposing forces.

"Son, when you get out there, you're going to be fighting one of the best fighting machines you've ever saw," he said. "These Vietnamese, Viet Minh, NVA (North Vietnamese regulars) have been fighting since they were children. They live there in the jungle. They know every rock, every stream, every mountain and they are very adept at holding their own. They've been whooping us all along."

The company that I was first assigned to go to in the 101st at Phan Rang had tragically seen this first-hand. Half of them had been ambushed a week before I got there and I was going to be sent to that same company that was nearly annihilated a week or two before I got to Vietnam.

There distinct differences among the type of Vietnamese people we encountered. A sergeant I'd known who had been a Ranger instructor and in Vietnam for a while filled me in on the situation. Along the coast were the Vietnamese, but they had moved down from China and North Vietnam. The people who had originally been there were smaller, stockier people called Mountain Yards. When the Chinese and North Vietnamese took over the cities along the coast, these original Vietnamese, the Mountain Yards, moved inland into the jungle mainly in the central highlands around Pleiku. The Mountain Yards continually fought the Vietnamese. The Vietnamese people were a small stature, about 5'7" at most, but typically 2-3 inches taller. Very seldom would you see one that had any meat on them whatsoever. They were very lean. Bones, skin, water and not much else because they had a hard life.

On the other end, the Mountain Yard people were shorter, but stockier. Their feet were near about as wide as they were long and their toes separated. The Mountain Yard people had lived in the mountains in the jungle so long, they had never really been civilized. When one of the first helicopters came into the central highlands near a Mountain Yard village, a woman came out with a straw broom made of grass and started trying to fight the helicopter. These people had hardly been exposed to warfare or the modern world.

The Mountain Yard men often wore a jacket or coat top with a loin cloth wrapped around their waist and between their legs. It was rare when they wore britches. Mountain Yard women wore a cloth wrapped around their waist and tucked in and reaching down to their ankles. They didn't wear a top over their chest, which was surprising to Americans. To see women, it was odd for us foreigners would even pay attention to a woman showing her breasts.

The Mountain Yards would fight for either the North Vietnam (NVA), but not for the South Vietnamese. They would also fight for Americans and be interpreters or provide support to a point. If you captured some of the Vietnamese, they would "chu hoi" which means they would turn and work with the South Vietnamese and go out as interpreters, carry weapons and fight right with you. With the country's makeup like that, you didn't always know who was actually loyal to the south or to the north.

At Camp Enari, Capt. Mayer told us the engineers said it would take three months to build a repelling tower. We needed to know how to repel out of helicopters and we needed men to know how to use the McGuire rig to get picked up by helicopters. The McGuire rig works with a rope hanging 120 ft. under the helicopter so you could feed the rope down into the jungle where a chopper could not land and pick up the LRP team. I told Captt. Mayer I could build a repelling tower in 3-4 days -- but I would have to "borrow" (steal) some materials, like telephone utility poles. Lt. Mayer said do it.

Around 1 a.m., I had a three-quarter-ton truck with some of my boys, who tied onto four utility poles we drug out of the engineer compound without being detected. The next morning we worked hard to dig 5 feet down into the hard red clay. It was like Georgia red clay up around Nankipooh. After that, we got a bunch of guys with the telephone poles on the truck and we walked that utility pole up into the ground, stood it up and had it level. We had to have it per-fectly straight. As we tamped the red clay around the pole, we saw an engineer captain and provost marshall pulling up and demanding to know who was in charge. Every one of those privates pointed to me.

I explained we were building a repelling tower, because we had to be operational in one week through properly training LRPs for jungle missions. They discussed our situation among themselves before telling me they couldn't let me build a repelling tower.

"You're not qualified. It's unsafe. We have requirements and reg-ulation about how to build towers," one of them said. "This engi-neering company's never built a repelling tower, so we've got to get diagrams and blueprints."

"Look captain, I've got 80-something men right here, second and third platoons. We've got a first platoon coming back from Recondo school. We've got fourth platoon that Maj. Malone's going

Tommy, at age 13.

Tommy with his cow, "Old Bossie," that he milked morning and night. In the background, the log cabin he was raised in, with mud between the logs.

Sgts Burton and Bragg demonstrate the Ranger "On Guard" position for hand-to-hand fighting. *Central Florida Fair, 1961*

Sgt Bragg throws Sgt Burton with a counter to the real strangle hold. *Central Florida Fair, 1961*

Rangers Performing for President John F. Kennedy at Ft. Bragg

Sgt. Bragg at the top of the rappelling tower next in line to rappel.

Sgt. Bragg is on the ground throwing a fellow Ranger.

Sgt. Bragg and fellow Rangers in formation for President Kennedy

The President's face registers his reaction to the demonstration.

1st Platoon "E" Company, 20th Infantry (LRP) after search and destroy mission. *Vietnam, 1967*

Vietnamese Prisoners of War, *1967*

Sgt. Bragg is standing at the far right in tiger fatigues. *Vietnam, 1967*

to bring here next Monday. The company's organized and we will be operational," I said. "These boys are going into the jungle and because you've got to get blueprints and don't know how to build a repelling tower, you're going to stop the war?"

I offered to build the repelling tower and have them send inspectors to check for safety. If they were unsatisfied, they could tear it down.

I thought it might take four to five days to build. In three days, we had the four poles up with 2x6's nailed in the whole front with spaces between then. We had one side boarded in with a ladder in the back. We had a frame around two sides of the thing where you could tie off your ropes and repel down the front. One side was open where you could just sit down and repel like coming out of a helicopter. We had a traverse tied to one corner, with a one-inch rope running out there going into the ground with a dead man for an anchor point. You have to dig a trench and tie your rope around the log and drop the log down in the trench. The rope would actually be around the log and it would just come out of the ground. You're not going to pull that log out the ground. Rangers learned all this in Ranger school, but as a Ranger instructor, you learned it over and over and I had been a Ranger instructor six years.

In three days, we had four pieces of plywood nailed on the back of that repelling tower, where we could project movie shows at night. Troops come from everywhere to watch movies up against that tower. You could repel down one side or the front. An engineer finally showed up for inspection. He walked around, looked at it, climbed on it, shook it and left. He didn't say he approved it or disapproved it, but no one made us tear it down.

I had those young boys out of the 101st coming off that thing looking like a circus: sliding down the traverse, 50 feet in the air, hitting the ground running. Then they would come off the side like a helicopter and then down the front. It was unbelievable how much attention that repelling tower got and how much confidence they had going up that high and coming down on a rope. They loved it and they couldn't wait to repel down again.

I thought I was so good. You always get the big head when you do a few miracles like that building that base camp. One of those private LRPs bet he could out-repel me.

"Son, you don't even know what you're talking about. You go ahead and start repelling and I'll start when I want to. You go ahead down this tower and I'll beat you to the ground."

My Ranger buddy Max Haney invented the slack jump. That's when you pull up half the rope and coil it up and then you hook into the rope, so the ropes only hanging halfway down to the ground in front of the tower when you hook it in your snap-link. It's rolled up on top of the tower when you jump, so you fall all the way down and about halfway the rope starts going through the snap-link and it slows you down. If you have the right amount of rope taken up, you'll land on your feet and never touch the front of the tower.

Well I had my rope coiled and hooked up and when he started rappelling down I let him get down about 10-15 feet and I jumped off the tower. The only problem is I took too much rope. I landed on that red clay in a sitting position and busted my L1 and L2 vertebrae and cracked my right hip. It knocked me out. I don't know how long I was lying there, but when I woke up, all these guys I'd trained were with all these paratroopers standing around looking down at me and calling for a medic. I told them I was OK and not to get the medic. The private, a LRP, had bet a dollar he could out repel me. He walked over to me, looked down and said "here" as he dropped a dollar on my chest as I rested on the ground with a broken hip and back.

I crawled around and got to my feet. I was in some kind of pain. I went to my bunk, because as long as I laid down on my back it didn't hurt. If I moved, it was really bad. Maj. Malone came down to ask me what happened and I told him I'd hurt myself slack-jumping, but I would be all right. He insisted I go to the hospital. Despite my objection, he sent his jeep over to take me to be checked out. It took an all day procedure to get me from Camp Anari up to Pleiku and the Air Force hospital. I got there at dark and was told I'd have to come back tomorrow morning when sick call was done. I'd been dry-heaving and throwing up from 10 a.m. to after dark that day, so I lied down on the ground beside the door to stave off the pain.

An old sergeant came out and asked what happened. I told him I had hurt my hip and back and could hardly walk. He took me inside for X-rays. I went to the room where they bring in wounded from the jungle. Tables were lined up with big bright lights in the ceiling. You could tell that they washed the blood and stuff off the tables with a hose pipe. After X-rays, I was put on a table where they do surgery. Then I saw a whole hall of doctors and nurses coming my way. I raised my head up and they told me immediately not to move.

"Just lie down. Don't move your head at all. Don't move anything," a nurse told me.

They talked among themselves before one doctor told them to be quiet and let him tell me.

"You have pieces of your disk, L1 and L2, away from your spinal column on the outside. We don't know what's on the inside, if the pieces of your disk or inside the spinal column and your right hip is cracked," he said. "You could be paralyzed. This is a very serious situation here."

The doctor explained they were going to keep me in bed without moving for three months while deciding if anything could be done. We're going to put you in a ward and you're going to lay in bed without moving for three months and they were going to decide if they can do anything or whether to send me back to Long Binh or to the

States. They started cutting and took my boots off and my brand new jungle fatigues with scissors.

"Whoa, whoa, whoa. You can't cut up my jungle fatigues! They're brand new," I protested.

"You shut up and lie down," I was told as they continued.

They cut all my clothes off and had me laying on the table naked with a sheet in front of mixed company. Now I have to admit I looked pretty good, but I didn't want to show all. They put me in a ward with about 60 guys. The nurse told me the next day that all the others guys there claim to have back trouble, but they knew I was the only one with an actual broken back. Then she reminded me to quit moving around and stop talking, though it is hard for me to be still.

I finally got the records from the hospital a few years ago. I thought I was in the hospital for two weeks, but I was only in the hospital for seven days. It wasn't the pain I couldn't stand, it was doing nothing that bothered me more.

I grabbed some clothes and left the hospital in great pain to go back to my unit. That captain and the nurse cried and begged me to get back in bed. I told her I just couldn't do it. I had a bunch of young men out there whom I'd trained. I was their Ranger instructor and I'd been their principal instructor to get them ready for war. I couldn't go back to the States and leave them here, even if I had a broken back.

I got a ride back to the company. Each bump hurt riding down those bombed out roads. When I arrived and got out the jeep, some guys saw me as I walked into the room.

"Even a broken back won't stop a Ranger," one said.

And the morale of the unit was greatly enhanced.

"You can't stop a Ranger. We're going all the way," I remember some of the troops saying.

After arriving back, I didn't have to do anything I didn't want to do because everybody knew I was in pain when I moved, but I was there.

The first platoon's sergeant was named Sgt Wilson They went out on a platoon-sized mission. A lieutenant called in artillery and had a short round that hit and blasted Sgt. Wilson nearly in two. He's still alive today, but he is carrying a colostomy bag and has had medical problems ever since. The next day, maybe because of getting blown up and other men getting hit with the short round, the platoon leader named Lt. Brown followed a blood trail up a hill while trying to kill the Viet Cong. The Viet Cong had probably killed a chicken and was splattering its blood along the trail to get soldiers to pursue them after they had contact. Lt. Brown was leading the platoon, running to catch what he thought was the enemy.

Instead he ran into a Chinese claymore (big round mines) set up by the Viet Cong. The mine blew Lt. Brown's head virtually off and it killed another man and wounded others. The first platoon came back on stand down, because they were in shock. Four to six of the men left the platoon and left combat because of the trauma of seeing the lieutenant blown apart.

Lt. Mayer and I went to identify Lt. Brown's body and the others. To see those men mutilated like that -- and I'd seen people shot before and seen dead people before -- to see what happens when you're hit with a mine as explosives cut through your body was a new shock to me. I've never forgotten that and I never knew I wouldn't be able to get that picture out of my mind.

The second platoon went back to McV Recondo school. I also went, but I didn't do anything except follow them around and do what I wanted to do because of my medical condition. We got back to Camp Anari where first platoon, still on stand down, was getting restless after a couple weeks off. One of the worst things you can do to troops is just let them sit around and think, even though these men have been through so much. The men in the first platoon were saying nobody was going to come in and take over the first platoon because they were going to run it. I was the ranking E-6 in the company and I was laying on my bunk when a soldier we called "Gingerbread" came in and told me that the first platoon is rioting. They had told the new company commander, Maj. O'Connell, who wasn't as forceful as Maj. Malone, that he wasn't deciding what to do.

I got upset when Gingerbread told me that, so I went to Maj. O'Connell and said I was the ranking E-6 in the company, that I was the first platoon sergeant and acting platoon leader and I would be running the platoon from then on. I told him I would have a formation out in the company street at 1300 hours. He could come out and see what happens. I told him thank you sir, saluted and left. He didn't say anything, so I virtually took command of the first platoon.

I walked into the first platoon and talked to the team leaders. One of them was Sgt. Burgos, who was with me at Okinawa in the 173rd. I told them I was the ranking E-6 in the company. I was the first platoon sergeant and acting platoon leader. I told one of the sergeants to have the platoon in formation outside at 1300 hours and I would tell the rest of the troops.

"If anybody has anything to say, step out the back door, because this is not a democratic army," I said. "The ranking man assumes command of the squad, platoon or company wherever it is, and I'm the ranking man."

Some of them started to say something. I set them straight before they finished.

"Step out the back door. I'll talk to you by yourself outside the back door. Don't say anything in here. You don't get a vote."

I came back from chow and told the first platoon how it was. In the meantime, Maj. O'Connell told me the first platoon would be going to operate out of the Oasis and operate near the Laotian border. I told them if anyone in platoon had anything they wanted to say, go between the barracks and we would get things straight. I offered to fight any one of them and all of them with a broken back and broke hip and feeling completely crazy. I look back on it and think, "What in the world were you thinking? What kind of idiot are you?" If I would have got in a fight I probably would have ended up paralyzed."

The platoon went to the Oasis and we reported to the unit there to begin operating. I would brief the teams and the unit we were attached to would brief them and coordinate with artillery. We'd coordinate with friendly fire and make sure we had all our equipment, then we'd insert the teams by use of three slicks and two gunships into a landing zone (LZ). They would move out and accomplish their mission.

While I was acting first platoon leader, I inserted every team that went in and was in charge in every extraction. For 75 missions, my broken body was in the chopper. A few times I was out of the chopper on the ground helping them shoot people, helping them get prisoners or picking up equipment while still under fire. I crawled under the chopper one time when the McGuire rig got hung up – the "donut" was hooked to the center under the chopper. The chopper was being shot at and I'm out on the strut, crawling directly under the chopper to retrieve the rig and got it, crawled back into the chopper, pulled it back up and untangled it out of the jungle and dropped it back down to the team. The harnesses on the McGuire rig had an ammo can full of grenades for weight when it would go down through the limbs to get to the team so they could get in the harness. If we had taken off with the chopper and went to a secure area and I had to get out and get it when it got hung up, it would have taken 30 minutes or more while this six-man team was out there fighting a company of VC. So instead, I crawled under the chopper.

All these years I've thought of that, because I never said anything about it. Recently, however I went to Louisville, Kentucky and there were 10 other guys that were in the first platoon. One of them, Mattingly, recalled that moment.

"You know, I never will forget that day when you crawled under that chopper and you were hanging under the helicopter getting that McGuire rig and getting back into the chopper under fire," he said.

"Well heck, I wish I'd known who you were and where you were," I told him. "I was trying to find someone to verify it so I could put it in my Ranger Hall of Fame letter." (That was about a year prior to running into Mattingly.)

After that first platoon, we got new replacements. One of the first missions we had out of the Oasis stemmed from intelligence on the Viet Cong. We were near the Ho Chi Minh Trail and there was movement, like one, two or three Viet Cong or NVA walking the trails. No large units had been spotted, but that was the reason they wanted us out there to find out exactly what was there, because there was so much activity.

They briefed us and we organized a team to snatch a prisoner. Mark Miller was a Spec-4, I believe, at the time. We had a brand new man on the team and they assigned him to carry the 20 pound radio. Generally, we always put the newbie with the weight or machine gun. In this case, they didn't have a machine gun, they had M-16s, CAR-15s and over and under (a gun with a grenade launcher under the barrel. You'd have an M-16 with a grenade launcher attached.) They were to land and insert them in the valley, then let them work their way up the side of the mountain as the trail was on the ridge at the top. We inserted a six-man team and by the next day or two they moved to the top of the mountain. They left four guys back 100-200 yards off the trail and two guys crawled up and watched the trail the rest of that day. They didn't see anybody. The team eased back down with the four guys and spent the night in some deep jungle brush.

They moved up to the trail in the morning. They had two men facing up the trail with a Claymore mine set near the trail and they were back off the trail about 10 feet, but it was thick. They had two guys on the other ends with Claymore mines set out and they were facing down the trail. The plan was to have two guys in the middle that were going to jump out and beat up the Viet Cong, tie them up, gag them and drag them off down to the bottom of a hill to an open area where they could be extracted.

They all got into position that morning about 0800 hours. As they stayed low with their camouflage and their Claymore mines set, they saw a fellow coming up the trail wearing a khaki uniform with a soft cap and an AK-47, shining in the morning sunshine. Then there were two other guys not too far behind him in the same uniform and a little space back, four or five more coming. They weren't really on guard, so much, but they were watching and looking and walking up the trail, making no noise. The trail was well worn.

The first guy walked by. The next two or three guys walked by. About the fourth or fifth guy looked directly at the team leader, seeing his eyes in the jungle. These two men who were going to snatch a team were only six or seven feet off the trail. Even though he was camouflaged, that NVA soldier looked him square in the eye in the vegetation. Immediately, he knew the guy saw him because he made clear eye contact. They blew the Claymore mines and the first six or seven guys disappeared. Then they started running. They heard the command that the Viet Cong gave, being passed from soldier to soldier down the trail and the command went back so far until you couldn't hear it any more. They didn't know if there was a hundred or 200-300 people. They didn't know how many these six men who were supposed to capture a prisoner had ambushed.

We could hear them running by listening on the radio. You could hear the bullets going by their heads. The radio operator was a new man on his first mission. All the guys were really new. They'd only been on two or three mission at best. Mark Miller, who lives in California, was running, as was the team leader. Miller heard the RTO screaming and begging. He had run into bamboo and vines and got hung up, literally stuck in the jungle. Miller ran back, snatched him out of the bamboo and vines and fell to the ground. Miller took off running. The Viet Cong were running down the hill shooting at them. They ran through a base camp where there were still little fires burning that some of his unit were at the night before. The unit was actually between them and the extraction point when they went up. They had just missed them somehow. When they came back, they ran right through their camp.

The team ran down to the base. We already had the extraction choppers in the air. I was in the command control chopper. Four of the men were together with the radio operator and they ran into this bottom end where elephant grass was. Elephant grass will grow six to eight feet high and it will cut you just like a knife. It slices like a paper cut, but elephant grass will cut your clothes and your skin. It's like razor wire and really tough to get through. The Viet Cong were still after them from the side of the mountain. The helicopter pilot was told they had four men here, but didn't know where the other two men were. The commander of the chopper, probably a captain or major, told them he wasn't going down to get them until all six got together. They weren't going to leave two out there and have to search for them.

"You go get my four men. If we don't get but four, we'll get the four," I said over the radio.

He looked around at me and I'm sitting behind him with a loaded

M-16. He decided to tell the extraction chopper to go in and get those four. The chopper landed about 50-100 yards from the team. When the the four men got to the helicopter, the two other men were sitting in it waiting on them. I just knew those two men weren't going to be very far from the LZ.

We flew back to the Oasis, which is the fire base. We went in to be debriefed by the unit we were attached to. This had been the first major contact for the first platoon other than when Lt. Brown was killed. The radio operator was completely battle fatigued. His clothes were torn up. He had cuts all over. The heel and sole of his brand new jungle boots had come loose while running. The other members of the team were bruised and cut up, too. Because of the team, we located either a company or battalion sized unit, which they were able to locate and, not annihilate them, but disrupt them and cause many casualties. As soon as the team had pulled out, they started putting in artillery and heavy equipment on them. That's how you use a LRP team. They're not to fight, but just gather information. On many missions, however, they couldn't avoid getting in contact and shooting up some people.

I talked to Mark Miller regularly over the years. He went on tohave 30 missions as a LRP. Most LRPs would burn out somewhere around 25 mission. Some made a few more and some made a few less. I had guys who made 30 missions, but you could begin to see change in them. No matter the frame of mind they had or how confident they were, you would see them start to doubt themselves after 25 missions, wondering: "Is this the one I'm not going to come back from?" It's just a different war.

Americans hadn't fought this way since the French and Indian War with Ranger Churchill. Then when Roger's Rangers fought the British. Mosby, Swamp Fox and Merrill fought out of the swamps in South Carolina against the British. So the LRPs of Vietnam go way back in to the Ranger tradition.

LRPs called themselves jungle rats because they crawled around on their stomach in the jungle among the deadfall, including rotten leaves and wood. Their biggest weapon was secrecy. As long as they were hidden and no one knew they were there, they were safe. As soon as they were compromised, they couldn't fight very long because they only had what they carried on their back.

With the LRPs, you may almost get as close an arm's length between a Viet Cong and you -- and he never knows you're there. You have your face all painted and everything camouflage as he comes walking by. Matter of fact I had one man on my team who got peed on. We were in the bush and the Viet Cong stopped right there and they broke for lunch. We were lying there and the man came over and relieved himself in the bush right on my man. I knew he couldn't move because he would get shot. You're that close to them in the jungle. Vietnam was a different war than most any other war, but the LRPs were the way to fight Vietnam.

One of the main things was about the dress, the clothing and the equipment. LRPs could wear anything they wanted, to a point. They could carry any kind of weapon they wanted to carry that we could get our hands on. We also had special equipment. We wore soft caps with the luminous tabs on the back. A luminous tab is about an inch long and half-inch wide. Often at night you wouldn't be able to see anything but those two luminous tabs on the back of the Ranger's hat in front you. If you're walking through the woods or jungle, you watch those two tabs as you feel yourself along on a real dark night. Sometimes I would take my hat off in my hand and as I walked I would lower my hat and the Ranger behind me would start bending over looking to see if he was going to step in a hole, then he would figure out what I was doing.

I'd have LRPs fall in before every mission and I would check them for their equipment. I'd have them jump and up and down and make sure they didn't make any noise. I'd check to see if they had the right amount of ammo and enough magazines. I did not require any specific amount of magazines or grenades -- it was according to the team leader -- but I did require each man to carry a Claymore mine. When you stopped at night, you could set Claymore mines out. Some team members would carry a 30-calibre machine gun. In most units, atropine syrettes were carried by medics. Those were like morphine in a toothpaste-like tube with a needle that screws on the end. The needle is covered with a plastic cover and you pull that cover off and stick it in a guy's thigh and mash it to put morphine in his leg when he was shot. Some of the guys misused the morphine. Some of them would be feeling pretty good sometimes.

You prepared before every mission to make sure you wouldn't make noise. We taped all our gear with friction tape or masking tape where it wouldn't rattle and make noise. We didn't take a bath for a day or two before we went out because they could smell the soap on your body. The food we brought wouldn't include things like fish, garlic, onions or kimchi because they're very sensitive, the Viet Cong, to their elements. A lot of them were born and grew up in the jungle.

LRPs had one guy who wore a helmet liner, not a helmet, because he could put his handset radio on the strap on the side of the liner where the chin strap would normally go. That way he could always have his handset on his ear. So these new phone earpieces you see sticking out of people's ears? That boy, Sgt. Strange, invented that back in Vietnam. He had his own little earphone. Sgt. Strange once fell out of a McGuire rig backwards, only hanging by his feet. It was a good thing he had that handset by his ear because he was able to keep screaming until he got someone's attention.

Most of the guys carried M-16s, the basic main weapon. Some

carried carbines. Some even had a pistol that they wore and carried. Some had sawed-off shotguns. I wore tactical fatigues most of the time, but there were jungle fatigues and some wore black pajamas because of the Viet Cong, who were mostly in black pajamas. You get those down in the village where the Vietnamese got their clothes. They were so loose and flimsy. I couldn't stand to wear anything like that out in the field because they didn't give you any protection. At least jungle fatigues had some strength to them and it wasn't like silk.

In the units we were attached to, NCOs and officers didn't like that the LRPs wore any kind of clothing they wanted to and the regular Army had to wear jungle fatigues, GI belt and their Army cap. You would have six-man LRP teams going this way and that all day and all night long. We were completely odd to the American Army in Vietnam and the people we were attached to sometimes didn't like us at all because we had little special privileges, but we took a greater risk than the other soldiers because we went out with six-men teams.

The enemy had been killing regular army units in the jungle as if they were walking around like elephants. They knew exactly where the Americans were. When we put six-man LRP teams out there, we were fighting them like they were fighting us. The bounty on a LRP was $10,000 for capture or confirmed kill. It was the same as an American colonel. They organized special teams in North Vietnam, Hanoi, and they trained them to go to South Vietnam and capture or kill a complete LRP team.

At the end of Vietnam, for every LRP killed, there was more than 20 NVA/Viet Cong killed face-to-face. This is individual kills, not calling in artillery or airstrikes. I lost only one man on 70 missions. That's like Spartans holding off the Persians at the pass there going into Greece kind of stuff. The number of enemy that died by artillery and airstrikes because a LRP team watched a valley, road, intersection or trail and called in artillery, airstrikes and gunships, would be 100-to-1 kill ratio.

This one LRP team made contact with that team and ambushed and killed them. On their bodies they found material showing their mission was to target LRP teams. They sent more than one team to South Vietnam, but we know one team was sent just to eradicate the "men with painted faces."

In Vietnam, it was everyday that you're not just fighting the enemy, you're fighting the jungle and humidity. You were always wet. If you stopped in certain places, you could have upwards of 50 leeches on you within five minutes and you wouldn't even know they were on you because you're tired, exhausted and you fall back to take a break. You stop moving for a few minutes while the point man goes forward to check the trail and you're lying there trying to get a rest and all of a sudden you got leeches in your ear, trying to go up your penis and trying to get into any cavity of the body, which is a big problem to get out. If you pull a leech off and his head stayed in, you're going to have a bad infection. But if you drop the salt or GI mosquito repellant on him, he'd turn loose and say uncle. One of my favorite things was to use a drop or two of mosquito repellant, Army issue, on a leech and watch him, because it would mess him up.

And all this came on a good day. Don't let it starting raining. The monsoons all brought other types of animals. It could be anything and everything there. You might be five or six feet away from somebody and not know it. You also had tigers, elephants, snakes, goar (a type of water buffalo) and monkeys of all types that could kill. The jungle was so dense and you were close to wild animals. A startled elephant once jumped up and ran by us. We didn't even know he was there, about 20-30 feet from us, when he rose up and started knocking down trees, making a two-lane highway down the side of the mountain.

For a man to volunteer to be a LRP and go out in the jungle 20 miles where some teams had never heard of before and take that chance, it takes a very unique soldier who is looking for excitement. It's someone ready to risk his life, not particularly for his country or his family, but for his fellow Ranger. Those guys with him depend on him to keep them alive and he depends on them. It's a bond that you can't build any other way. Football and basketball players form bonds, but when you go into combat with six men, you live, work and die together.

I ran that platoon for nine months. I lost one man on radio relay. You might say I trained the first LRPs beginning in 1967. There were units before then that would leave teams of four to seven men behind or let them doing what LRPs were doing, but they were doing it on their own. They didn't know we were eventually going to have units of LRPs. LRPs were in Vietnam from 1967-1971. At the most, we had 1,600 LRPs at one time in Vietnam in 1969. It's unbelievable that in those four of five years, the most you ever had was 1,600 at one time and still have such a history in Vietnam. The Viet Cong called us the men with the painted faces, but American soldiers called us jungle rats. We'd crawl around in the jungle, but may not move 50 yards on a whole mission.

After three or four months, when I was attached to the fourth battalion 173rd and we had a lot of good action at Tuy Hoa, I was told to report to Col. Cleland, the battalion commander. He told me day after tomorrow, the corps commander is going to be here and he wants you to brief him on what we've done with the LRP. I said I was only an E-6 and couldn't brief a three-star general.

"Use that Georgia charm on him and you'll be all right," Col. Cleland told me.

I briefed Gen. Rossen about what we did and how we operated by hiding, observing and trying to survive. Three months later, most every division in Vietnam had a LRP company. It wasn't E Company 20th Infantry LRPs any more, Airborne, it was Charlie Company 75th Rangers. Now I'm not going to say first platoon with an E-6 acting platoon leader changed the makeup of the United States Army, but to me, that's what it looked like. I know we had other LRP platoons over there and other people acting as LRPs two to three years before that. But that was actually the first LRP company organized, along with one other company organized three or four months later. And it was my platoon that the corps commander came down to learn more about our operations.

I reunited with some of the men from my platoon decades later in Indiana in 2014. Our gathering was recounted in a story by a local newspaper, which also talked about the formation and impact of the LRPs. Along with myself, those who were part of that reunion were Mike Burgos of Florida, Tim Mattingly of Ohio, Mike Kemble of Minnesota, Richard Spratley of Missouri, Garry Dalton of Kentucky, Everett Cress of Indiana, Dave Bechtold of Pennsylvania and Don Chambers, Randy Hayes and Ed Hazelton, all of Texas.

The man most unlikely to go in the Army, or even get a job cleaning up bathrooms, had grown to lead men in combat and save hundreds of lives -- even though he still couldn't read very well. That was one reason I never wrote my men or myself up for awards. I was afraid people would find out I couldn't read or write. So my men went without getting Silver Stars and Bronze Stars they surely deserved, over and over. I think about how my ignorance and fear of being found out caused my men not to get the awards they deserved. Anyone of them knew they could write each other up for awards and get them, but I was the man in charge.

Then there was the Tet of 1968, when we were at Tuy Hoa. This was the Vietnamese New Year, their big holiday like the Fourth of

July. Without Americans knowing it, they had planned to attack every city in South Vietnam and take them over. The day before that night of Tet, a team leader of mine, Sgt. Milton, observed men coming out in a valley in formation moving south. After 30 to 45 minutes there was 100 or more men in black pajamas or khaki uniforms moving from the west of Tuy Hoa down to the river that led into Tuy Hoa.

We called in artillery and they put a company of 173rd troopers out there. Though they didn't see very much, it disrupted that battalion from attacking Tuy Hoa that night. Along about dark, I heard a radio relay on the hill right outside Tuy Hoa. One of my men on radio relay was watching the south China Sea and looking over the town of Tuy Hoa from a high hill. He looked up the beach -- I guess being a LRP he was always looking -- and he saw these troops marching down from the north to the south heading straight for Tuy Hoa, located on the south China Sea shore. The radio operator told me and I called for support, as the gunships went up the beach, they saw these men and shot rockets and machine guns at them. It disrupted the battalion-sized unit moving toward Tuy Hoa just at dark. They ran into the jungle and the choppers had search lights trying to detect them. That night, when they attacked Tuy Hoa, the attacking force was disorganized to such a point until they broke into the outer perimeter. That's the farthest they made it because first platoon E Company 20th Infantry LRPs had saved the town of Tuy Hoa by being the eyes and ears of the commander.

The next morning I rode down Highway 1. They had 89 Viet Cong laying along the side of the highway. I'll never forget that. You see one or two dead people and that's bad enough, but when you see 89 lined up, it's different. And this is just the ones the Viet Cong didn't drag off or hide. They were very good at getting their dead and wounded off the battlefield before daylight and hiding them so you wouldn't know how many you killed.

When I moved to Blackshear, Georgia there was a man living next door to me named Don Thomason. He was superintendent for Atlanta Gas & Light Company. He and I were talking about Vietnam when he said he was in Tuy Hoa during the Tet of 1968 as the Viet Cong broke through the perimeter and shot guys in the next foxhole he was in, but that's as far as they got. He said he and another guy in the foxhole were scared to death. That was a line the Lord drew to save his life. Here it was 30 years later when I find a man who was alive today because of what we did. Every other major city in South Vietnam was overrun and captured by the Viet Cong in Tet '68. The things they did to the people in all of these cities was horrendous, including torture, especially the people who worked with American troops. But they didn't overrun Tuy Hoa.

All the terrible things you saw and hear living in war in Vietnam made the light-hearted stories stick out even more. And, because it's me, there were a few.

The first platoon I took over after Lt. Brown's death had left their equipment at a South Vietnamese camp. They had put their gear, piled up around the center pole in this tent. They had bought an orangutan, but it wasn't an orangutan, it was a macan. He had a big head, big teeth and his hands were longer, his legs were short but his feet were like hands. I took some MPs out to this South Vietnamese compound where these soldiers left their equipment. I went up to the tent and opened the flap to walk in when I heard, "AAAAAHHH-HH!"

Man, I couldn't believe it. I fell on the ground and rolled around.

"What in the world nearly got me?"

They had tied this macan, later we called him Frank, with a chain to the top of the center pole. He could run all the way around on their equipment. They left him food and water. It had been about two or more weeks, so he had run out of food and water. His neck was raw where he'd tried to get loose, but he was still protecting that equipment. I don't know if he knew he was doing that or if he just didn't want anyone getting close to him while he was tied up. I opened the flap for another shot at it as he growled at me.

"Look here monkey. My mission is to get this equipment and I will accomplish my mission. If you don't get out the way, you're going to get hurt."

This was a bad monkey here, so I eased toward him and hit him in the side of his head, knocking him down. He was in a weakened state when he then crawled on my leg and whimpered. Before I knew it, he was sitting on my shoulder with his head right next to me. I got him loose from his chain and tied a belt around his waist. By the time I got that monkey straight, they had taken the tent down and had everything on the truck. I got in the back of the jeep with the monkey. One man said he wasn't getting in the jeep because the monkey was still aggressive to everybody but me, because I'd given him some food and water. He was still jumping around, acting crazy.

We drove away in the jeep and the monkey jumped out and got his leg run over. I climbed up on the deuce-and-a-half, the big truck, where I sat on top of the canvas with my foot on the top of the truck. The monkey would run down and scream at the driver.

We finally got back to the rear and kept him tied to the tent, where he was getting healthy. We left Dragon Mountain and went to Tuy Hoa, where we built a tent. We had Frank tied outside there on a chain. He would play with a stick. If guys got too close walking by, Frank would grab you and he would bite you. It wasn't anything to see him have a Ranger by his boot and two other Rangers trying to pull him away from the monkey. The only person who could do anything with him was me, because he remembered I'd hit him. I'd go out there and tell Frank to turn them loose and sit down. Frank would whimper away. I told him if he didn't behave I'd put him back in the jungle. That's probably where he wanted to go anyway.

We went to the mess hall. Soldiers have a tendency when they serve in a unit, then go to another unit, to later request to go back to that unit. There were some guys in 173rd that were there when I was there. The mess sergeant was a big ol' guy who came in to greet me.

"I heard you were here, Nankipooh. You still think you're bad?" he said, cutting up.

Two or three sergeants that knew me came in and were laughing about Rangers and asking if I was still eating frogs, grasshoppers and chewing on roots like I used to do.

"You think you're bad, but I have the baddest paratrooper in Vietnam right out back and you won't mess with him," the mess sergeant told me. "I got a bad motor scooter out here."

He had a dog from Siberia. It was huge, like a rottweiler on steroids. He had wide shoulders and a big head and was fed steaks out of the mess hall.

"He looks bad," I said.

"He is bad," he replied. "Won't nothing mess with him."

I told him I had a little Ranger down yonder that was pretty bad himself, even though he wasn't as big as that dog. I said he's got four feet or four hands. I'm not sure.

"Well this right here will mess him up," the mess sergeant boasted.

"I don't know. It might be a close one," I told him. "That little Ranger is tough and quick."

He said he would bring his "paratrooper" down that evening to find out. There were already guys betting money. We got down there and Frank is playing with his stick, looking around, scratching like didn't have a worry in the world. Up the road came the mess sergeant with maybe 30 paratroopers who had heard about the showdown. All of a sudden the dog got about 300 meters away and stopped. He smelled something and started growling viciously. He was scratching the ground and peeing wherever he could. It took two men to hold that dog back.

Frank hadn't even looked at the dog. He looked at the ground, at me and the sky. The dog was coming closer as they held him back. Others were getting their bets ready, hundreds of dollars on this thing.

"We don't have to let them fight," I told the mess sergeant

"Are you scared? Your little Ranger isn't so bad after all is he?"

"The Ranger isn't scared. He's not even worried. The dog is the one cutting up."

Finally, the bets were down. They turned the dog loose and he jumped into the air and landed, then the next time he jumped he landed where the monkey had been. The monkey was now on his back with the stick. He had grabbed the dog under his privates with the other hand, he had a foot around his eyes and his other foot somewhere else and he was biting him. He was working the dog with that stick. This monkey was working him like a Singer sewing machine. It was like poetry in motion, hanging on top of this dog three time bigger than he was. The dog's growls soon turned to whimpers and he spun around in desperation.

That dog finally realized he couldn't stay there any longer, so he took off. The monkey was doing good until he got to the end of the chain and it flipped him off the dog and he landed on his feet with his stick in hand, screaming at the dog.

"That dog will be in Hanoi by tonight if you don't get him," I said. "He's not going to look back and see what got him."

There's a lot of stories about that monkey, but that was one of the funniest things. It got to where we couldn't take him anymore because we were attached to another unit. We left him at the base camp, Camp Anari. They got a Conex container (an iron box,

10x10x10 cube with two doors on the front) and took the doors off. They had a place for his food and water and a stick inside where he could climb. Everybody came by to mess with the monkey to see if he would react. This guy who thought he was bad, got down there one night in the beer tent and got him some fire water. He said he was going to whoop the monkey. The only men who ever did that were me and Frank Moore, a first sergeant, who knocked the monkey down like I did. So this guy jumped into the container, drunk, and Frank beat him, nearly killed him. And soon he was gone to the hospital.

Now I don't know first-hand that this next story is true, but Lt. Mayer told me this not long after we first got Frank. Maj. Malone said they were going to take the monkey to the general mess. The commander of the Fourth Infantry Division was leaving. Every time a commander left, they would throw a big party and a new commander would take over.

They had Doughnut Dollies, the Red Cross women, and they all looked pretty good. They would have them give doughnuts to the troops to help morale. The general was having his going-away party with special steaks. We hardly ever got those kind. There was all kind of wine and whiskey. The officers took turns talking and patting each other on the back. Maj. Malone told someone to go get Frank. Lt. Mayer says, and he was there, they brought Frank in and everybody thought he was so cute. He was looking around and he liked beer. They also gave him a piece of steak. Then he jumped up on table and ate the steak. They thought it was cute.

About that time, he decided he was going to run the table, stepping in everybody's plate. Frank made it up to the general and they say the monkey took the general's wine, sipped it and spit it all over everybody. He didn't like the wine and threw it down and went back down the table. Folks yelled to get the monkey out of there. Maj.

Malone got Frank and as he was pulling him away, the monkey grabbed a beer and a steak and yelled back into the room as they pulled him through the door. Phi Mayer said that was the truth with Frank disrupting the general's go-home party.

Nobody but LRPs do stuff like that. I knew this one lieutenant that pulled a good one.

This one Ranger instructor, a lieutenant from the Florida Ranger Camp, came to Ft. Benning and they had a big party at the officer's club. This officer was married to a good-looking German woman, though she was a little bit loose. She was out there playing her role and everybody was after her, but she was married to a major or colonel. She was a doll, but she was too friendly. Well this lieutenant Ranger was thinking she took a liking to him and had picked him out. Being a Ranger, he wasn't going to be denied, no matter the difficulty or the danger, he was going to try something.

After the party, he went around to their house. He was caught sneaking in to see her and got in a fight.

"Son, what were you thinking? You can't do that kind of stuff!" I told him.

But that's part of LRPs and Rangers. When they think of something, they do that. Any daring mission or something like that. There's no telling what they might do -- and I was the worst of any of them. That lieutenant was a novice. He wasn't very good at being a fool. A man once told me I was a fool.

"Nah, I'm not an average fool. I'm a thoroughbred."

If anything, I'm going to be the best.

When it came to a mission, there was no foolishness. That's one reason my men and I are alive. I lost no men in my two tours while I was in charge of the mission. The first time I had 75 missions and 30 missions the second time with a Recon platoon.

I was actually surrounded all night on my first mission. The Viet

Cong were coming across the field with flashlights. My team was on the side of the hill. We had been moving along ridge line three or four days. We watched this field all day. Down at the bottom was a river. Right before dark I was watching from the side of this hill and saw this big tree. I said we were going to move over there and spend the night in the brush under that tree. So we went there and under it was as clean as we could tell even though it was getting dark. We put a Claymore on the tree and put one on the ground. I told everybody to go to sleep and I would stay awake as long as I could, then I would wake up someone and they would take turns staying up for an hour, then wake me up again. As they slept, I looked out there through my camouflage in the brush at the corner of this open grassy field and spotted a man with a flashlight. Then another 30 or 40 feet was another man with a flashlight in Vietnam walking across the field. They were walking straight towards me from below in the field. By the time the first man got 100 yards from me there was about 15 flashlights spread out across that big field. That's some first mission. I woke up the others and called to tell the base about the flashlights and to get artillery ready. I doubled-checked my coordinates.

They didn't know exactly where we were, but they could see the Claymore mines. There wasn't a way to get around behind me. I didn't know that was a weigh station. They had been using that for a place to come and spend the night under that tree. I did pull the team out of the field beyond the tree and set up behind, back in the brush and the brambles and vines and rocks where you couldn't get in either which way.

When they came closer, one man shined the light in the tree. He saw the Claymore mine and immediately turned the light out. I heard him bark and order. You heard people move around and then silence. I told my men not to shoot.

"Throw your grenades and they won't know where we are, but if they pinpoint us, we're dead."

Few people had worked as LRPs, so they probably thought we were a company or platoon in position along that woodline. They pulled back into the field. All night long we were wide-awake, trying to stay quiet and alive. They would throw sticks and rocks in there trying to get us to give away our position. We never blew the Claymore mine, so they knew not to go down there and there was no way for them to get behind us. I got under my pancho on the radio to adjust artillery.

"This is my location, my coordinates. If they get in here to attack us and we can't fight them off, I want you to fire artillery on my location and give us everything you have."

I figured maybe we could filter down through the rocks and maybe some of us would survive. If there were five or 10 people between those flashlights, there was a herd of them. All night long they kept trying to get us to shoot.

A chopper came to pick us up the next morning. We went down the side of the woodline as it approached. When it came in about where we would have been if we continued our mission, all kind of stuff opened up on those choppers. The gunships fired back as the chopper picked us up and we later put a company back out there. That was my first mission: all night long, scared to death and unable to shoot.

After we made it back, we seemed like heroes. After the debriefing, Phil Mayer told me something interesting.

"Tom, you didn't have any support. I couldn't tell you last night, but the artillery unit we coordinated with that was going to support your operation was ordered to move yesterday afternoon," he said. "We had not one bit of artillery. If you'd gotten in contact, you would have had it on your own until we got gunships out there -- and they're not good at night."

War is hell. You can shape it anyway you want to. When things are happening, things are happening. After it's over, you may not have ever realized how bad it was and how lucky you were that you didn't end up losing an arm, a leg or your head. I think back at that and sometimes I get mad. Most of the time I just laugh.

CHAPTER 6 -- DOWNTRODDEN
IN DAHLONEGA

My first year in Vietnam had been successful overall. I boarded the Freedom Bird to ride back home on a high note from Vietnam.

I initially received orders to the 82nd Airborne at Ft. Bragg, but a week later those orders were amended to send me to Ranger department. This time, though, it didn't feel as thrilling. I had already spent six years as a Ranger instructor. That's a lot of days of being up before daylight, doing Army daily dozen (calisthenics) such as push-ups, sit-ups, side-straddle hops, squat jumps and running up to five miles, only to follow that up with two hours of hand-to-hand pit, then two hours of classes and two more hours of demonstrating bay-onet, followed by a couple more hours of classes before getting chow ahead of road marches lasting up to 10 p.m. or 1 a.m.

I had enough of that and I thought my body deserved a break. When I showed up to Ranger department, I was told to go to the hand-to-hand. There was a Ranger class starting and they wanted me to demonstrate that day.

"I'm not even here yet!" I reminded them. "I'm still on leave. I just came in a day or two early."

The sergeant major and I had a very pointed discussion and I told him I wasn't going to be at Benning. I was going to be at Dahlonega or down at Eglin Air Force Base at the Florida ranger camp, one or the other. I'd had enough of Ft. Benning, even though my home of

Nankipooh was just 10 miles north of Columbus. He agreed and I got orders to Dahlonega -- which turned out to be a miscue on my part.

I got my little Fiat smoking as I departed. We didn't make any money and the car would hardly run during the drive to Dahlonega. The mountain Ranger camp sets about 30 miles past Dahlonega up through Camp Road where it dead ends. I arrived at the cantina with my car still smoking. There were 10 or 15 Ranger instructors outside at the place where they could get a beer or Coke during break.

"There's Tommy Tucker, the chicken plucker, the mean so-and-so," said Sgt. Doug Perry as I got out of the car.

All the guys had heard of me and I had heard of most of them. We talked for a while about how I was stationed at the mountain Ranger camp after coming back from Vietnam. In the middle of shooting the breeze, a Sgt. Blackwater said he wanted to see how bad I was. I told him I wasn't really that bad, just a hand-to-hand instructor. He told me to get ready because he was going to take me to town tonight.

After I went to the barracks to bathe, I saw his car pulling up. It looked about as terrible as my vehicle -- smoking, popping and barely running. I hopped in and we went down Camp Road up to Suches, which is over the mountain up toward Tennessee. There was a concrete block building on the left with a big sign that simply said, "Beer." I told Sgt. Blackwater to pull in so I could get a drink. He said he wouldn't, because they had thrown him out last week.

There were logging trucks around the side and gravel all around. It was a pretty rough-looking place. I insisted he take me there. I said he could stand at the door and count them while I threw them out.

I swaggered in and encountered this big, ugly mountain man. He must have been eight foot tall, with hair growing out his T-shirt, up under his chin and growing out the sleeves around his arm pit. It looked like three beards hanging out from that boy. He was humped over as he asked what I wanted. I asked for a beer, but biggun' had already decided what he was going to serve me.

"You Rangers come down here..." he said as he lunged. That knocker grabbed me by the seat of the britches and nap of the neck and ran me through the screen door

"One!" Blackwater said as I hit the ground.

"You're not supposed to count me!"

Unfortunately, this start to my stay at mountain Ranger camp would be typical of the time yet to come.

I was eventually assigned to the patrolling committee, which had a rope committee for repelling and mountaineering. They had a big cliff south of the camp, created from a rock face they had blown away for Ranger students to learn repelling and how to tie knots. On the face of the cliff there were X's here and there. When I asked why, they said that's where a Ranger got killed. One fell over and hit the ground. The other X is where one broke his leg and that other is where one broke his neck. They ran these classes through year after year and a lot of people trained on that cliff, which is about 50-70 feet high.

The patrolling committee walked patrol, where Ranger students were given a mission. You would appoint one man as patrol leader. The patrol would vary from 10 men to 40 men, but generally you had a 10-15 man patrol with one in charge. He would have to go through the complete patrol. The first thing he would issue is a warning order, which would set up exactly the things he would do between that time and the time they departed to go on patrol. He would appoint assistant patrol leaders, aft patrolleaders, machine gunners, radio operator and he would give them time to draw their equipment, ammunition, weapons and then meet back for the patrol order. During this time of planning, you'd coordinate with the friendly frontline and the artillery and any other supporting unit that may be involved in your mission.

The leader would go through the complete mission in the patrol order, which you called a five-paragraph field order. You would tell each man what he's to do at all times on a patrol: order of march, actions at danger areas, actions at the objective, what to do if you're attacked from the front of contact or ambushed from the right or left, all signals to be used, flares, whistles or whatever you were going to use to start the assault or reassemble. The in-depth patrol order would take you about an hour. Every man must know exactly what he's going to do, what he's going to carry and how he's going to act at different points during the mission.

Then you have rehearsals for the actions at the objective or danger areas. Finally, you have final inspection and then you "kill" that patrol leader because that was the planning stage. You appoint another Ranger and you're given a list to grade on that patrol. Then the next Ranger student would be in charge of the patrol and he would have them going through friendly front lines or being inserted into the LZ, what to do when you go through friendly front lines when its dark. You go outside the friendly front lines into enemy territory a few hundred meters and you stay there for 15-20 minutes until you get accustomed to the night noises, you get your night vision and you get accustomed to your surroundings at night, because Rangers love to operate at night or in the rain. That's when the enemy is most likely to be unsuspecting of any visitors.

You also graded the navigation part, which is very important. They should be able to read a map, follow a compass and go from Point A to Point B to get to an objective. Once he gets near the objective, you "kill" him and you would appoint yet another Ranger and he would go through the actions at the objective. You'd reassemble, disseminating information to make sure all the elements of the patrol would know exactly what was at the objective. You might have a support team, an assault team, a snatch team. A snatch team would be two to three men that would get a prisoner and knock him out and bring him back. An assault team would assault through the objective. Support team would be set up to support the assault team and give covering fire. They may not see all the things happening at the objective: How many people are there? What kind of equipment, vehicles, weapons, defense or lighting system they might be using. Then you pull back and disseminate information and make sure everyone on patrol knows what you accomplished, so if only one survived and got back to friendly lines, they would have all that intelligence about the enemy to report.

Then you would "kill" that leader and appoint another one for the navigation and return trip back through friendly front lines, then you'd have a debriefing. The worst part of the whole deal for a Ranger instructor walking lanes on patrol is when you'd have to write up everyone of these guys you graded and either pass him or flunk him. A Ranger instructor has a lot of responsibility to flunk a guy on patrol in Ranger school. If you flunk two patrols, you were out. Yet, my problem was being able to write these people up. I always used no more than three and four-letter words to describe what they did. I really had a hard time writing them up because I wasn't educated. I'd turn in my report and a lot of times it was rejected, so I would have to go back and write them again and correct misspelled words.

I did that for about five or six months. Then the leader of our patrolling committee threw me a curveball with my next instruction.

"Sgt. Bragg, the next mission they will go on is going to be a week-long mission, but they did not get survival class at Ft. Benning," he said. "I know you taught survival for years at Ft. Benning., so you're going to give a quick survival course tomorrow morning to the whole Ranger class so that when they meet the friendly partisan and he gives them live chickens, carrots, potatoes, onion and rice, they will know how to prepare a meal in a jungle."

A friendly partisan is a guy that would live in that area. He would be a civilian and in the mountains we worked with mountain men -- ones wearing overalls, with big long beard and an old mountain hat -- the real thing. We would recruit people that actually lived up there to go in and meet the Ranger students and make like they were friendly to the American cause, working against our enemies.

The students would be getting a chicken for every third man and the company would get vegetables and rice. I was to teach them how to kill the chicken, cut him up and cook it all in a canteen cup. That's virtually saying you're going to starve. If they build a fire on the ground and put a canteen cup up there and you have 30-40 guys with a canteen cup around a fire, then someone comes around and turns over someone's food-filled canteen, things get testy.

Not only did you have to kill the chicken, but you got to pluck it and you don't do that without boiling water. My Ranger class started at 4 a.m. because we had to wake the Rangers up an extra hour early when they only got two hours sleep each night anyway. When Ranger students came into the classroom, they came in stomping their feet, filing in and getting behind their tables, standing there growling and making all kinds of sounds. The Ranger class commander comes forward and reports to the instructor and then gives the command: "Seats!"

The night before I had to have me a chicken, so I told one of the NCO's who lived in the mountains. A lot of these guys were born and raised in Dahlonega and went into the Army and then were assigned back to the mountain Ranger camp. A lot of them were old farm boys. This guy had a lot of chickens, hound dogs and hogs and things at this house. He agreed to bring me a chicken I could kill and show the students how to prepare him. The next morning he showed up with an old hen that was on Medicare. She had chicken lice with feathers missing all around her behind and her neck. She was a piti-ful-looking chicken. I asked why he brought me this ugly chicken. He explained he simply reached into the coop because they were on the roost. You can't catch a chicken unless they're on the roost at night. A chicken in the daytime will run and carry on.

Now if you want to get somebody to help you be an instructor, you need to get a young Ranger who just graduated Ranger school. He is assigned there with the old Rangers and a lot of these old Rangers had been in combat in the second World War, Korea and been on the Bataan Death March. They had been to Vietnam and had been in combat. These young Rangers want to fit in, so they're try-ing to be tough and act like the old boys. So I got me a young E-5 ser-geant and told him he was the assistant instructor and was going to help teach survival in the morning. I gave him instructions for when I told him to come out with the chicken.

"You're going to bite that chicken's head off, but you're not real-ly going to do that," I said. "You're just going to grab the chicken and put his neck in your mouth and twist his neck and jerk it."

That's the way we always killed chickens back in Nankipooh. You just wring the chicken's neck and jerk it and the head will come off. Then he flops around and blood flies everywhere before you catch it and put it in a pot of boiling water. I'd gotten a bucket of boiling water from the mess hall and brought it over for my class demon-stration. That's the only way you're going to pluck those feathers off that chicken. Just dip him down in that hot boiling water because that makes those feathers turn loose.

There are many ways to kill a chicken. I know people back home would tie the chicken's legs on the clothesline and cut the head off with a knife. They jump around a long time after the head's off. They can jump around 40 or 50 feet with no head.

"Demonstrator, post!" I yelled as my assistant ran out with the chicken.

He was growling as he stopped, put one hand behind his back holding the chicken with his right hand. I told the class what he was going to do. He got the chicken's neck in his mouth, but the old hen was so tough with the mites and all on her that he chewed and acted like that and twisted and jerked on her head and all he did was come out with a mouth full of feathers. And the chicken was still squawking around.

Some Ranger students were already getting sick. Four in the morning isn't any time to be messing with a chicken. I finally grabbed the chicken and wrung its neck before boiling it to pluck the feathers. The main thing you have to remember is when you cut the chicken and you look inside, there's a thing called a gall in there -- a green thing by the liver. If you bust the gall, it will taint the chicken and you can't eat it. Save the liver and the heart, but get rid of the gall and the guts. Then you cut the chicken into parts for three Rangers. Two Rangers get chicken legs and I don't know who's going to get the neck, but you got to split it up and put it in the canteen cup to boil the meat, vegetables and rice.

I wished the Ranger students a lot of luck, because I knew it wasn't going to work. Most of them turned the canteen cup over with dinner in it. Some of them fought each other because they stepped on the stick and upset the fire and knocked the cup over. In short, it was an exercise in starvation for the Ranger students. But to have a class on survival that fast with few training days, it's very hard to teach them something. Normally in survival we teach them to kill a goat or young calf and to cut it up for the whole company to cook it or roast it. A chicken, however, is a funny thing to fool with.

I remember how hot it got during the Dahlonega summer when you're climbing up mountains carrying a pack.

We used to go to an Atlanta Braves baseball game every once in a while, back when they always lost. You could take a NPRC-25 radio and you could turn it over to the TV station and hear the game broadcast. On patrol, the instructor just wears a rucksack and whatever he wants to take. It usually weighs nothing. A Ranger student has to have cold weather boots, extra clothes, ammunition and other equipment, plus then this guy was carrying an NPRC-25 plus an extra battery. It weighs 19 pounds plus the battery weighs about four or five pounds. The entire pack weighs about 100 pounds or more.

I offered for one Ranger to carry my light rucksack in exchange for letting me haul the radio so I could listen to the ballgame. So all the way from the base of the mountain up to the Tennessee Valley Divide, I carried this Ranger student's 100-pound rucksack to listen to the Braves on the radio. It was in the afternoon and the game was tied. When we made it to the top of the mountain, I was soaking wet from sweat. The Ranger who was walking with my light rucksack was smiling. I was listening to the ball game as we get to the top, where there was a road and the Rangers' mission was to observe it and come back to patrol. It was still tied and I had to turn the radio to their frequency in case they got any calls once we were up top and report in that we were in position. While I was fooling with the Ranger students, the game went off. I didn't find out until two or three days later who won, after carrying that rucksack up that mountain. Momma never did say she raised any smart kids.

There were times, however, when I intentionally tried to look out for Ranger students. One patrol in which I was grading Ranger students showed the stress that a student goes through after a few days or a week out with little food, two or three hours of sleep a night. It was early in the morning, just before day when a Ranger told me he had left his rucksack at our last stop during the night. A rucksack has 100 pounds of equipment and clothes. This Ranger was sitting down in the mountains and walked out with his harness and his weapon, but left his ruck sack.

I told the Ranger students they had one more day and then they would go back to the mountain Ranger camp. I told him after we get back and I write up the Rangers I'm grading, I'd go back in my car and follow the route from last night. If I found the ruck sack, I'd give it to him the next day. I had finished the write-ups and had gone well beyond 24 hours without sleep as I drove up across the Appalachian Trail and the Tennessee Valley Divide. I parked my car and walked the mountains on our route. Sure enough, there was his ruck sack. I took it back to him.No one ever knew he lost it. If they would have found out, they would have probably flunked him out of Ranger school immediately and he would have had to pay $200 to $300 for lost equipment that was in there. So you see, I wasn't all bad.

About my third or fourth day in mountain Ranger camp, I went downtown to get a meal at a restaurant right off the square in Dahlonega. When I came out of the restaurant, this car pulled up in front of me and a girl said to get in. I looked in the car and she looked pretty nice, about 25 years old and not real skinny. I got in the car -- which I should not have done. As she drove outside the city, I learned she knew all about me.

"You're new at the camp. You were a Ranger instructor at Benning. You're well known."

I asked how she knew.

"We girls in Dahlonega know about all the guys at the camp."

She drove up the dirt roads of the mountains. There was a rock wall on one side and a drop-off on the other. She pulled into the recess of a little cove where a stream came out of the mountain. She and I were getting sort of friendly for a little while when a policeman shined a light into the car. She started calling him bad names and cursing at him. Turns out, that was one of her boyfriends.

The officer told me to get out of the car with no clothes on and walk back to Dahlonega. I asked to get my clothes, to no avail.

"You like to get undressed? You're going to walk to Dahlonega by yourself," he said.

Now that was embarrassing. He was standing there telling me to walk faster and keep going when this girlfriend grabbed his car keys and threw them 200-300 yards down the side of the mountain. So then I really started walking fast. She sped away up the hill as I continued down the hill.

I was cold and those roads were full of rocks. It was not a good place to be walking at night, especially with no clothes on. I got about a half-mile down and saw headlights coming up the hill. In the mountains, you can see car lights a long ways off because when the car faces out over the valley, the lights go a mile or two against the other mountain over there as it swings around, so you can see if something's coming a long time before it gets to you. And something was headed my way -- another police car.

"What you doing up here naked?" he said as he rolled down his window.

"I'm trying to get to Dahlonega. Would you give me a ride?"

The officer said he had to go up to take care of some business and would be back to get me in a little bit. There wasn't anywhere I could go. He wasn't gone too long before the girl who brought me up there was coming down the hill in her car. She told me to get in. I hesitated just a second before jumping in the back seat and putting my clothes on. When she got me back to Dahlonega, I got my car and went to the camp. I stayed at the mountain Ranger camp for a solid week before I ever ventured to leave again. You see, such is my life. I was not the average soldier at all. I was absolutely in all kind of trouble. It certainly didn't seem to get better there.

I did not have a good reputation with the sheriff and police in Dahlonega. They had their eyes out for me. Anytime I came through town they'd get behind and follow my car, motivating me to get back to camp quickly. They knew me from the episode I had with the police officer's girlfriend. That was a factor from a mishap one time on patrol.

It always felt like a freezing winter when I was walking a patrol. It rained, snowed and rained some more. On patrol, you have to check the Rangers ever so often because they are so tired and worn out that they can't think properly after a week or two of this training. They don't get any rest or the right kind of food because they're pushed to the limits. If one of them gets frostbite on their nose, ears or fingers and toes, they blame the Ranger instructor who's grading that patrol. So you have to check to make sure they don't have frostbite.

On this one patrol on a freezing night, we got to our objective -- an old house people had lived in on federal property because this is part of a forest preserve on the Appalachian Trail. People who lived all through those mountains were able to live in those houses until they died. When they died, it went to the federal government. We sometimes used these houses for objectives.

That night, our objective was a two-story house. There were aggressors in the house and they had built a fire in the fireplace. When my patrol got into position to assault the house, there were about two or three blanks fired. It was so cold the weapons wouldn't even shoot. When the aggressors saw us coming, they just ran to their trucks and took off because they were freezing too.

The Rangers were getting really cold and pitiful. We'd been out there two or three days, so I told them to go into the house to stay for a few hours to get warm and keep from getting frostbite. Some Rangers went upstairs and tore boards off the wall and brought them down to build up a good fire in the fireplace. They were all lying asleep by their gear when I looked over and and saw the boards over the fireplace smoking. I went outside the house and saw it was on fire in the second floor. The old chimney had a hole in it up there and it burned the second floor. There was a creek next to the house, but it was of little use since it was frozen solid.

I got the Rangers out the house. We stood out there near the blaze until daylight. We were the warmest patrol in the whole country that night as the house burned down.

The house just happened to belong to the local sheriff.

I had burned down the sheriff's house, but it wasn't all my fault. When we went down to meet up with our relief, a captain put me under arrest. He put me in a jeep and took me back to camp. He said I was restricted to my quarters.

They were going to court martial me for burning down the house. Everything in the mountain Ranger camp went through Ft. Benning. Gen. York was Ft. Benning post commander and his son was a Ranger student on that patrol. It was just before Christmas, so after the son graduated from Ranger school he was home with his family. They mentioned that they were going to court martial a Ranger. Lt. York told his father, Gen. York, he was on that patrol and that it was smart to take us in the house to get warm rather than stay out in zero temperature and get frostbite. Plus, the fire was burning when we got in the house. So those charges were dropped.

The reason I got in trouble and accused of so much is because I was always ready to take a challenge or do whatever. People knew I wasn't afraid of anything and a little bit dumb.

But I wasn't the only person like that.

We had a sergeant major and a first sergeant from Ft. Benning who was reassigned to the mountain Ranger camp. They were reassigned because they had beat up a private or two at Ft. Benning. Sometimes if somebody, like an officer or enlisted man is in trouble, the Army would move them out of that camp to another place where it's harder for the person they harmed or the thing they did wrong to catch up with them.

This sergeant major thought he was a bad motor scooter. When they first got there he had everybody at the mountain Ranger camp assemble. All the enlisted personnel in the classroom. He got up on the stage and started saying he liked to "drink, fight and f---" in front of all the enlisted people. I stood up and told him he wasn't much of a sergeant major to get up and talk in such a way in front of the troops. That was a sad accounting of a senior NCO. Naturally, my standing up in front of the whole enlisted camp didn't go over with him very well.

The sergeant major was quite huge and his first sergeant was an average-sized guy. They would run together and had been assigned with each other many assignments, according to them. That way they protected each other. One Saturday, this NCO asked me to take him down to Dahlonega to a party because he didn't have a car. I agreed and took him to a trailer park. I found out this is where a Spec-5 lived with his beautiful wife. He was a cook directly under the sergeant major and first sergeant.

After dropping the sergeant, an E-7, off at the party, I drove back to the mountain Ranger camp. About three or four hours later he called asking me to pick him up. When I arrived, he invited me in to have a drink. I declined the drink, but went into the trailer. There were these guys sitting around, with the Spec-5 passed out. I heard a young lady in the back bedroom with the sergeant major telling him to leave her alone and get his hands off of her. I went down the hallway, opened the door and he was purely trying to rape the girl. I told him he was just a stupid idiot.

As he was trying to put his clothes on, I walked back to the living room where the other guys were. The first sergeant said if I step outside that the sergeant major would whoop my behind. I told him to come on. When I opened the trailer door and got to the second of the wrought-iron steps, I noticed out the corner of my eye the first sergeant was trying to kick me in the head from the door of the trailer. His foot grazed the side of my head as I ducked. I grabbed his leg and snatched him down the steps. He was lying on the ground with his head on the steps. I was beating on him and his head was bouncing off the iron steps from the impact. I looked up and the sergeant major was standing in the door telling me to stop whipping his first sergeant. I told him he was supposed to be down there with me, not up there trying to rape another man's wife.

Sergeant major wouldn't come down and join the fight. So that shows how bad he was. He'd beat up privates at Ft. Benning but he wouldn't fight a sergeant in the mountain Ranger camp. The first sergeant had gotten loose from me and had picked up a brick in the yard and said he was going to hit me with a brick. I started after him and he ran with the brick in his hand. That was something. This sergeant major and first sergeant with a brick in his hand running from somebody.

I got in my car and the sergeant I had come to pick up was already inside. We went back to the camp. I can tell you my stay in the mountain Ranger camp was one of the worst for a short time with the problems I got into. I don't think anyone could have gotten into any more problems in two and a half years than that. My time there was not productive.

A few other things happened and the colonel threatened me with a court martial. The colonel had gone to Florida and embarrassed the Florida Ranger Camp commander. The Florida Ranger Camp commander was doing something that our commander found fault with it and made him look really bad. I kept a jar there for those who wanted to give money to a needy family. There was a woman down on Camp Road that had five or six kids, who were sometimes seen running around the yard naked by a home that had no electricity. So when a captain from the Florida camp came through our area grading as a TAC officer, he noticed us bagging groceries in the PX while running Ranger students through quickly. This fellow knew I was a Ranger instructor working at the PX. That night he had a company formation and he ordered the Ranger students to write statements saying I was ordering them to put money in the jar or I would flunk them on patrol.

I had ended up in the middle of their dispute. That captain saw an opportunity when he spotted me in the PX. I should never been working in the PX as a Ranger instructor anyway. I just have a whole lot of energy and I knew I needed to be working or doing something all the time or I'd get in trouble. That's why my best two years were in Vietnam.

I was told to report to the colonel's office that night along with Sgt. Lee. We had no idea what was going on. This TAC officer was getting back at our colonel for embarrassing his colonel in Florida. The TAC officer had the Ranger students lined up outside the colonel's office, bringing them in one at a time. Out of 240 Ranger students he got 13 to write statements he had ordered. For me to get a Ranger student on my patrol, to grade him, is like one out of a thousand. At least one out of a hundred. And then for me to flunk the guy because he didn't put a tip in a jar for a needy family is absolutely crazy. However, the colonel bit into it and they brought the Rangers in and all of them said I had asked them to put money in the jar for the needy family, except the last one, who said, "Sgt. Bragg said if I didn't put money in the jar, he was going to flunk me on patrol."

I explained I would never say something like that. The colonel said he was going to give me a court martial, which truly had me upset and scared.

As things got closer to court martial, those against me rewrote the statements the Rangers had done and this captain operations officer signed the Ranger students' names to the new statements. Matter of fact, they rewrote the statements three or four times to make them the way they wanted them to go to court martial. Here I am about to get thrown out the Army with 15 years of service and no retirement. It was just a terrible situation. Everybody knew I was down.

Then came a spark in my favor. A Sgt. Rump brought me some vague, but good news one day at the PX.

"Sgt. Bragg, you don't have anything to worry about," he said confidently. "I could tell you, but I don't want to, but I guarantee you this is going to backfire on the colonel and the captain."

I wasn't convinced quite yet. Sgt. Rump said if I promised to control myself, he would tell me what happened. Sgt. Rump was the TAC NCO, while the other TAC officer was the one ordering them to write the statements. Sgt. Rump told me after the captain got the Ranger students in formation, he ordered them to write a statement that I had coerced them for monetary gain. He continued pressuring them even outside the colonel's office.

"When you go in there, you better not wimp out. You better stick it to him," he said. "Say that he forced you to give the money or he would flunk you on patrol."

Turns out, all of them told the truth, except the last guy. Rump said the captain threatened action against that last Ranger student if he wimped out. That TAC officer had every one of those students under his control, since he is the one who ultimately passes them. I could flunk him on patrol and the captain could decide he would pass him because he is the TAC officer for the Ranger class.

"Plus, they rewrote the statements here at headquarters. I know three times that clerk in there retyped them and the captain (operation officer) signed the new statements with the Rangers' names,"

Rump said. "So when you go in to get a court martial, you're going to destroy the colonel's career and the captain's career because I'm going to be there to tell them what really happened. You and I went to give that woman groceries out of our pockets."

That old mountain woman walked around with no shoes on. It was terrible. Thing is, the colonel went by her home everyday going to work. All those officers and all those NCOs and nobody stopped to help that woman and her kids.

After Sgt. Rump shared those details, I came unglued and went up the hill as others tried holding me back. I went into headquarters screaming for the captain. The captain, for my luck, was not there at the time. I asked this Spec-4 clerk how many times he rewrote those statements for the Ranger students and how many times they forged the students' names to make the statements the way they wanted. I was screaming at him and he was scared to death. Then the colonel came out of his office and I told him off.

"You're going to give me a court martial? If I messed up, I'm man enough to take it -- and you're going to be man enough to take it too."

Two or three weeks passed before the captain came back to me.

"Look, we have to give you some punishment. I talked to the colonel and he said he would give you a company grade Article 15 and only a reprimand and we'll take this off the books," he said. "If we go to get a court martial, you never know what's going to happen."

I knew that was true, but I told him they had already put me through the ringer and we were going to get a court martial. I was going to have Sgt. Rump in there to explain they had the students lie. A few weeks went by and the captain came back with the same offer again.

"Sgt. Bragg, will you please take this Article 15? It won't be on your record. I guarantee it."

"No sir. Nobody should be treated the way I was treated."

Then he came back and pleaded a third time.

"Ft. Benning says we have to do something with this situation. Will you please take an Article 15? I give you my word as an officer that it will not be on your record and it will be over," he said. "The colonel will give you his word as an officer and a gentleman that this will be a reprimand and he'll just say he chewed you out and that'll be it."

I was growing tired of the ordeal. I finally agreed to the Article 15 just to end it. I later went to headquarters and reported to the colonel's office. The captain was there. He had me sign the Article 15.

"Consider yourself reprimanded," the colonel said with little else.

I asked again about it going on my record.

"No, sergeant. It will not go on your record," the colonel said.

Back in 1968, if you had an Article 15 and you left that unit, that Article 15 was forgotten about. Starting the same year, however, if you got an Article 15, it followed you in your 201 file. They started keeping better records on people. I eventually went back to Vietnam without thinking about it anymore.

It wasn't until years later it caught up to me.

While working as a recruiter, I had eight years seniority as an E-8. Gen. Goodson, commander of the recruiting command at Ft. Sheridan saw me at a laundromat. (The general knew me personally and I later went into the Recruiting Hall of Fame under him.) He told me I was going to be promoted to an E-9, something he knew as president of the E-9 board. A few weeks went by and Gen. Goodson found me back in the laundry with a different story.

"Do you know you have an Article 15 on your record for soliciting money?"

"No, sir. My efficiency rating is 100% ever since I got over my first few years in the Army. Everything is max."

"I know. I didn't believe it, but you have an Article 15," he said. "They threw your records out and I would look at them and put them back in and they threw them out again. So you won't be making E-9."

This wasn't just about pride in promotion. Missing out on this cost me and my family an untold amount of money. In retirement, I would have been drawing the E-9 pay instead of the E-8. I've paid for it after all of these years, because two officers lied to me – and I won't call their names to protect the guilty. That's a sad case when you have officers blatantly lie to you. But if I had not taken the Article 15 and went to court martial, I'm sure it would have finished their careers. The colonel was caught in between, because that TAC officer had him pumped up to believe that I was guilty of doing something wrong, when he was really trying to get to the colonel through me, to be fair to the captain and teh colonel.

To say my tour in Dahlonega was just a regular tour, well, it was truly a terrible tour for me.

After two years and a few months, I was given orders back to Vietnam. I loved the mountains. I loved Dahlonega. I loved Ranger school. In my opinion, no matter what profession you're in anywhere in the world, you're going to run into people who will do anything to protect themselves, no matter if it hurts somebody else. When the sheriff's house burned down, I didn't light the fire. It was the aggressors' error in a house they had been using for years as an objective there, but I got accused of burning it down.

My time in Dahlonega was not to my advantage.

And that made getting sent back to Vietnam seem like a relief.

To be fair to the captain and the colonel, I really don't know how the Article 15 got in my record. But it sure looks that way.

CHAPTER 7 -- SURVIVING A SECOND ROUND IN VIETNAM

I received orders back to Vietnam around 1970. I flew in there like the first time, except I knew what to expect. I really wasn't as scared and I was more aware of what was going on. When I got off the aircraft, the people getting on the aircraft to leave Vietnam were passing us. This captain, a Ranger, saw me.

"Sgt. Bragg, the war is over. Don't get killed."

He got on the plane to come back to the states. I went through the replacement process.

I was sent to Chu Lai to the 23rd Infantry Division. They kept you at the replacement center for two or three weeks, then sent you to a jungle school where they have to refresh you about what to expect in the field. Immediately, I could tell that the people there had very low morals and morale was at rock bottom. No troops seemed to be interested in doing their job. They were just there, spending time, getting by with as little as they could. I was assigned in a tent -- a wooden floor, wooden frame with a tent spread over in. There was an E-7 pay clerk and this guy was drunk and had a case of beer under his bed. They said he'd been lying there three or four days. You'd hear him at night pop a hot beer and lay right back down drunk. This went on for about a week.

I talked to the first sergeant and he said I should get some privates to carry him to the shower and give him a bath. This guy was still drunk, but I had four guys who picked him up, took him to the shower, turned on the water and scrubbed him. He was on the floor drunk, an E-7 in the Army, who did not want to be in Vietnam and was more or less refusing to do his job and go where he was assigned to go, even though he had a rear job at the division headquarters in Chu Lai. That's absolutely unbelievable disrespect for the uniform, for his job, for the Army. It was just a completely different Army than I had know the first trip to Vietnam.

The protests with the hippies in San Francisco and Oakland outside the base and news articles had caused this to become a terrible place, where the motto was, "I don't want to be the last American to die in Vietnam."

After processing in, I was assigned to the first of 52nd 198 Infantry Brigade. I was on the truck with about 15 privates. They were dropped off on the street outside the headquarters of the first of the 52nd battalion headquarters. The reason there were no other NCOs or officers on the truck was because most of those guys had already called ahead to friends and got a rear job. When we got to the replacement center, the senior NCOs all went in different directions to talk to somebody about getting a job in the rear somewhere. One of the NCOs asked me if I had a job somewhere.

"No. I go where the Army assigns me. I'm a soldier," I said.

"Don't you have some friends at division headquarters or somewhere?" he replied incredulously.

"I'm sure I have some buddies in rear jobs, but I'm not looking for a rear job," I told him. "If they assign me to one, I'll do it."

"You're going to go to the field," he warned. "You're going to be in a company and walk around that jungle with a bunch of newbie draftees and you. Your odds of making it are slim."

The 15 new recruits on the truck were mostly draftees, also known as McNamara's 100,000. The Army had lowered their standards. McNamara was secretary of defense, I believe that was his title, and they authorized to put in 100,000 CAT-4s. Remember, when I went into the Army I made a 28 of 100. Well a CAT-4 is between a 16 and 32. Thirty-two to 60 is a CAT-3, where most people fall. They lowered the standard so they could get more people in the Army to get more people to go to Vietnam. They dropped us off in front of the battalion. I'm standing out there around 10 a.m. with these 15 young boys, scared to death, just got to Vietnam with no idea what to expect. Somebody hollered out of one of the hooches.

"Sgt. Bragg, is that you?" I turned around. "Tommy Bragg! Come here."

It was Maj. White, executive officer of the first of the 52nd.

"Our prayers have been answered," he said.

Maj. White got on the field phone and called LZ Stinson, the firebase where the first of the 52nd was stationed. LZ Stinson was the top of a hill out in the jungle. There were no roads to LZ Stinson. You had to come in by helicopter or walk. It was about 15 miles from Highway 1 or Chu Lai.

What they'd do is go out with a bulldozer and try to scrape down the top of a hill and make it as level as possible. Then they would dig a combo trench all around the top of that hill, so you could get into the trench in firing positions and walk all the way around and come back to where you were without getting out of the foxhole. Beyond that, they had razor wire and booby traps. They had bunkers all around the top of the firebase. On one end they had a resupply pad, where the hill leveled off into a saddle. As you approached the resupply pad, you'd see it had TWA in big letters, but when you got closer to the sign, it was written in small letters, "Teenie Weenie Airlines." On the other end of the hill was another ridge sticking out with a smaller landing pad. It was a VIP pad.

Maj. White told me Maj. Getz was on the phone and wanted to

talk. He had been the Florida Ranger Camp commander. He and Maj. White knew me well from Ranger school. Maj. Getz was so happy I was there.

"We've been praying for somebody like you. We got to have you here."

He told me to go immediately to LZ Stinson. I didn't have a weapon or equipment. He said not to worry, because they had all I needed at Stinson. After talking briefly with Maj. White, I went out to the resupply pad with my jungle fatigues and got on a helicopter by myself. I flew to LZ Stinson and landed on the VIP pad. Maj. Getz was there waiting for me. I saluted him and reported. He brought me to the TOC (Tactical Operation Center). Maj. Getz told me two weeks earlier that a recon platoon hit a booby trap and it killed the sergeant running recon, a guy that was a very fine NCO, and it killed eight guys in the squad and wounded eight more. The blast was so terrific that it blew up the Claymore mines in their rucksacks and the grenades on their harnesses.

Recon platoon, what was left, had been on stand down for two weeks. We had about 15 men of the original 30 or 35. A platoon usually has 42 men, but you usually run a bit short. Someone's in the hospital or someone's on R&R. Maj. Getz was briefing me about recon platoon. When I had taken over first platoon of E Company 20th Infantry LRP, the same type of thing had happened to me before.

I got another 20 guys in to recon and started training them to operate. In this case, instead of sending out six-man teams, with me being the platoon sergeant and acting platoon leader, I was in charge of the platoon on all missions. After two weeks I talked with the operation officer, a captain, and Maj. Getz and I told them I wanted to go out on a night raid to hit a village. They disagreed with it and said it wasn't a good idea because the Viet Cong move at night. In

Vietnam, the nights belonged to Charlie and the days belonged to American forces because we had the firepower.

My proposal was to go out, walk off LZ Stinson about midnight, then move around to the west and go south and hit a village at a place you always got sniped at, ambushed or shot at, but there were lots of rice paddies and hamlets and quite a few people lived there. Even though Maj. Getz and the operation officer disagreed with my night raid, I had trained a platoon I thought was ready to go out. We moved off the firebase about midnight and went down the hillside trail. It was very dark at the bottom. Two or three of my men said they weren't going because they couldn't see and they mutinied on me. I told them to sit and wait until we got our night vision and then we can start moving. They said they were going back up the hill to LZ Stinson. I had to grab them and wrestle them around there. I finally got their attention and we sat down there about 30 minutes until we got accustomed to the night.

We moved to the west a little bit and then south. We got just about to the village we were going to go in around 0300. As we were moving alongside a rice paddy dike, to our left front came a platoon of men back to back. Full rucksacks, weapons in the perfect formation. On the road coming out of the village we were going to raid, this platoon was choagying, not running or walking, they were choagying. This whole formation was moving in unison like you'd never seen before in a parade field, but they were nearly touching each other and they were moving rapidly.

Our point man froze. Our compass man froze along with me.

"Oh my God, don't let anyone behind us make noise or fall down," I thought.

I could tell that group of men was very professional, well-trained and highly-motivated troops. Wherever they were going, they intended to get there before daylight. Many a day I've thought about if we had been just a few minutes earlier, that we would have been on the little trail going in while they were coming out. And with those new guys, I'm sure we'd all been wiped out. So I thank God for letting those boys try to mutiny on me back there. All things work together for the good of those who serve God.

When the group passed, we moved up and I set my machine gun at the edge of the village. I sent in the first man to the first hooch front door. The second man went to the back door because they had little tunnels dug out behind the hooches where someone could crawl out and get away. The third and fourth man did the same at another hooch. The platoon continued to go into the village until we had every hooch covered. I called for a red flare from the artillery. When that red flare went across, they fired illumination. Illumination is an artillery round that burst in the air and it comes on a parachute and has about a thousand candle light power. It lights up nearly like daylight. By now it's 4:30 or 5 a.m. By the time we had people out of the hooches, we had 27 Viet Cong laying out there on the ground when the sun came up. Some were caught in the hooches and some were caught crawling out the back.

After the sun came up, we started getting sniper fire from the east. We returned fire with the machine gun crew and we took this group of male prisoners moving north back to LZ Stinson on a different route. We stayed in the rice paddies and the areas where the Vietnamese walk, because everything was booby-trapped. We maneuvered around and were getting fired at again from a wood line and some of the guys just started to run to the wood line across a flat rice patty. I shot some rounds over their head and told them to get down. I called artillery and adjusted the artillery to the wood line. They fired for effect. A lot of rounds landed over in the wood line and the sniper fire quit.

We got up and proceeded to our northwest around and walked

back up on LZ Stinson. You should have seen the men in that battalion when we started up that hill with all these prisoners. You were lucky to get one or two prisoners. In my first mission, here we were with 27. The only bad thing is, we later found out the prisoner we had walking point to make sure we weren't led into any booby traps was blind. I had wondered why he kept falling down. We didn't have an interpreter for us and this guy looked like he could see. He was big for one of the Viet Cong. That's the kind of thing that happened in Vietnam.

After the debriefing, recon platoon had a lot more confidence, more pride and it was able to get better morale. Then I had guys from the line companies coming to me wanting to get into recon platoon. I had some real crazy guys coming asking to join and there were one or two really good, smart guys. So recon platoon became pretty effective after that. We had quite a few missions. In one special mission we had been out in the field two or three days when we ran into some Viet Cong and had a firefight early in the morning. We killed three of four Viet Cong. They said another Viet Cong was going to die from his wounds, but he wasn't dead. I told them to wait until I got over there.

This man was sitting there, crying. He had been shot in the hand, lower part of his chest, his leg and the side of his head. He was crying, "Buku ita," which means "a lot of hurt." He said his hand was buku ita. I said, "my Lord have mercy." He was really shot up and still alive. He was nothing but skin and bones, weighing maybe 100 pounds. I figured he may have been high on opium or some other drug for him to still be up and talking to everybody.

I moved on down because they were chasing more Viet Cong. I told the guys to stay with him and we'd send a chopper to dust him off and get him to the hospital. We treated their wounded like we treated our wounded, at least that's how we did it when I was in charge. I did not allow someone to mistreat a prisoner or any Vietnamese. We got around the hill chasing the other four or five Viet Cong and I caught up with the front part of my platoon. We were strung out and headquarters kept calling how many kills I had and what was going on. I told them we were in hot pursuit. They told me the man died and we cancelled the dust off. When you see someone suffering like that, it's hard not to help them out of their misery. I don't care if it's the enemy or an American soldier.

We ran over the hill and down to partial hedges and bushes there. It was really thick jungle. We ran them down a hill and as we were going, we were joined by a platoon from Charlie Company with a lieutenant in charge. They got in line with us and started sweeping down the hill toward the river. We got down to the opening where the Vietnamese took the water buffalos across. Now D company was in a defensive position on the other side of the river. When we came out in the open around 10 in the morning, we were wet and our clothes looked black. We were shooting at the Viet Cong that ran into the river. D Company was shooting at us.

We hit the ground in the open and the helicopter pilot told my radio operator it was friendlies. At that time I got up and ran to each men and just about had to grab each one to make them quit firing because there was so much noise going on that I had to run all the way the length one way and then back the other way cross the line into Charlie Company platoon to make them quit firing. D Company was still firing. Then the colonel landed and ordered everyone into the river. Maj. Getz ran into the river with the troops. Everyone was down in the river and I'm walking around where I put these two injured guys into the colonel's helicopter to take them to the hospital.

I looked around on the ground and there wasn't hardly a place where there was two or three inches where the turf wasn't torn up.

I don't know how we didn't all get killed. God had something else for us to do for us not to be killed that day. We were lucky not to be killed. These are the things that happen in war. We couldn't find the Viet Cong that went into the river, so we reassembled and were picked up and flown back to LZ Stinson.

The recon platoon is the colonel's little honor guard more of less. It's his reactionary force and his special volunteer unit. They have a thing called eagle flights. You'd have three companies out and one company on the firebase. So at all times, one company was on the firebase around the perimeter and they would stay there three days and then they would take them out and pick up another company and bring them back. Four or five choppers would shuttle them back for rest and relaxation, to heal up and reload equipment. When they came back on the firebase, the ammunition they've been carrying was usually dirty. The hand grenades are muddy with the pins rusting. When they came back, they would drop all that explosive stuff over by a building, an ammo dump, and get new ammunition the three days they are on the fire base. After a while, you would accumulate a huge pile of explosives of all types on the fire base.

Maj. Getz told me he wanted me to blow up all the old ammo on the fire base. I told him somebody drawing hazardous duty pay was supposed to blow it up. I didn't know much, but I knew that. I was on combat pay. He said he was the battalion commander and he was telling me to blow it up. The operation officer was drawing hazardous duty pay, but he was afraid to blow up these highly-sensitive mines and things with blasting caps, C-4 and detonation cord that was all ragged, yet still highly active.

On this firebase we had an old three-quarter ton truck. It had no top, no windshield, just a steering wheel sticking up with only seats in the back. They used this truck to haul supplies from resupply pad around to its destination on this one circle road. They had one boy from Alabama, a mechanic, assigned to drive the truck.

I had a 10-man detail load the explosives on the truck, ride them down the side of the hill from the resupply pad and stack them in no man's land down the side of the firebase. It took all afternoon, about 10-15 trips, to haul this ammunition and highly-sensitive explosives down the hill to a washed-out, rutted road. I got down there and I set a time fuse for about 15 minutes. These were non-electric blasting caps with a fuse lighter and a time fuse, right into Claymore mines and TNT. I set another one for about 20 minutes on the other side. That boy from Alabama and I got in the truck and went up the hill. I think the whole battalion was on that side of the firebase to see this Fourth of July extravaganza. It was about an hour before dark and 15 minutes went by and nothing happened.

One guy pointed out Viet Cong who were spotted stealing the explosives from our pile on the side where I had the 15 minute time fuse burning. The Viet Cong had sneaked out of the brush right next to where we stacked this stuff. I don't know how many, but they were running in there grabbing these explosives. Maj. Getz and I looked at each other.

"You know if it doesn't go off, you have to go back down there and set some more charges to make sure it goes," he said.

"I got a trick for you," I replied.

About that time the 20-minute fuse I set on the near side blew up. It blew things in the air 200 to 300 feet and then those items exploded mid-air. Everybody was ducking because those rounds and rifle grenades were firing across the valley, shooting at people. I immediately asked Maj. Getz to get me a team. I was going to go back down there and see how many Viet Cong were killed. It was already getting dark, so I got some volunteers from recon and we took off on foot.

We got down there and found six Viet Cong blown apart and a blood trail leading off where there were more who were blown up and had been dragged away. They don't know how many in all were killed in my demo explosion. I was killing Vietcong -- and nearly killed everybody on the firebase -- when I was trying to get rid of ammunition. That shows you what a Ranger can do. A year before, an ammo bunker on a firebase, not Stinson, blew up in the 23rd Infantry Division. I don't think any Americans were killed, but there were a lot of them shellshocked and messed up from the great explosion.

When I got to this recon platoon, there were two men in recon who were guarding a prisoner. They had him in a Conex container, an iron box where you put supplies to ship. They kept him locked up at night, but the daytime they would go down and get him, let him see them load a .45 and the other one would rough him up a bit. They'd put a .45 to his head. While the other guy was roughing him up, he would unload the .45, and then he put it to the guy's head and pulled the trigger. They'd twist his arm and beat on him. When I got there, they had moved this prisoner back to Chu Lai through the channels, but they kept him out there for some reason on LZ Stinson. These two men had harassed him beyond what they should have done. When he got back to Chu Lai, this Viet Cong was at the hospital. He talked to some of the Vietnamese and they told him he could bring charges against the soldiers who mistreated him on LZ Stinson. He did just that against two guys in recon platoon. The soldiers would go back to HQ every two or three days to talk to their defense counsel, then come back to LZ Stinson and operate in recon platoon alongside the other soldiers who weren't being court martialed for harassing the enemy.

Understand the picture here: I've got a platoon of men and two of them are being court martialed by the enemy. Two guys who could go to jail because they beat up a prisoner. The other men in the platoon were saying, "What do you want me to do? If I hurt the enemy they may come back and sue me or press charges and I go to jail. I thought I was here to catch or kill the enemy." I don't think there's ever been an Army or country, anywhere at anytime that ever prosecuted their own men for hurting the enemy. So that made it more difficult to get the job done.

When a company was in the field and they got in contact with a unit of Viet Cong or NVA, they would load up recon platoon in helicopters put us in right on top of the Viet Cong. You knew where the enemy was in bushes or a valley or behind rock. We would get out right among the Viet Cong. That's kind of exciting. We did that on numerous occasions.

I had many missions and patrols. I was on a mission when one of my men moved to the edge of the military crest of the hill just to go to the bathroom. An American platoon down at the bottom of the hill saw him and thought he was a Viet Cong, so they started shooting at him. When I was down the ridge a bit, I went out over the edge and looked down to see what the shooting was about. My man was trying to get into a little hole about 18 inches deep. Rifle grenades and bullets were hitting all around him. He was down in that hole and there were only a matter of seconds before they were going to hit him because it was only about 250 to 300 yards. I ran out over the edge and started waving my arms. I thought I could get them to stop firing. Well instead of them stop shooting, more of the guys in that platoon joined in the shooting -- this time at me.

My man got out of the hole and started running back over the top of the hill. Once I saw he was already safe I tried running for cover. I only had my harness and weapon with me. As I went to jump over a bush, a blast from a rifle grenade hit right behind me and lifted me over the bush. I hit the ground, rolled and came up running back to my position. When I got there, the RTO said that the company in the valley is wanting to call in artillery up here because they're saying this place is loaded with Viet Cong. They said they blew one to pieces with a rifle grenade and the other one got away. They thought it had blown me to pieces because I had disappeared.

I had to get on the phone and tell them they couldn't fire artillery up here. They were shooting at us and I was the one they shot in the back with the rifle grenade. There I was offering my life to save a guy that was doing something he shouldn't have been doing. We were supposed to be hiding on top of the hill where American troops in the valley were moving around. The idea was that when the companies would move in the valley, the Viet Cong would sneak up the hill where we would catch them. But no, he had to compromise the whole operation by going down there and letting that line company think he was Viet Cong.

I'd been the platoon sergeant about seven or eight months and had not lost a man. A Lt. Billups came in and he was told by Maj. Getz to follow me around and keep his mouth shut while learning everything he could. I would go around at night and check on the troops. He was with the third squad, which was a rough bunch. I knew some of them smoked pot. I didn't know what else they did, but I knew they did some of that. I walked in one night and they were all high. I just looked around and made out like everything was OK and left. A lot of guys smoked pot in Vietnam. Some of them were among the best troops. As long as they did their job, it was sort of overlooked, but the lieutenant was right in the group.

We got a mission to go north of LZ Stinson and raid a village at night. I began drawing things in the sand to brief the platoon. For each mission, I issued a five-paragraph field order that covered everything from all signals to be used, all coordination with the artillery and mortar platoon, pre-planned concentrations along the route, rations and weapons to take, actions in danger areas and objectives and how to reassemble if someone got separated on the route. I had all this drawn out on C-ration boxes and I used sand pit on the ground showing exactly where we were going. You could about see the village from LZ Stinson.

Our mission was to go just north of Stinson and raid a village about a mile or two from the firebase. I got the platoon together and started issuing the five-paragraph field order. Lt. Billups, however, said he wanted to run the patrol. He had been on three or four missions already, but it sort of surprised me he wanted to take charge when he didn't have to because he had me there to do it. I said fine, if he thought he was ready to take over this platoon, then he could get them prepared.

"OK boys, we're going to go out tonight about 0100 hours, hit the village up here and come back. I'll see y'all at 0100," he said.

"Whoa! Wait a minute!" I said in near disbelief. "You're not going to issue any order, route, plans or signals?"

"No Sgt. Bragg. These are seasoned troops. These men know what they are doing. We don't need to go through all that bull."

"Fellas, I'm going to tell you this. I've run y'all for over seven months and not one of you are dead. Now do you want the lieutenant to be in charge or do you want me to be in charge? It's your choice."

The rowdy third squad started hollering, "We want L-T! We want L-T!" L-T's is what they called lieutenants in Vietnam.

The good guys, the first and second squads, just kept quiet. They didn't care or didn't have an opinion.

"OK. You want him? You got him," I said.

Sure enough, we didn't do anything until 0100 hours. We assembled and walked off the firebase. We went around the westside of the firebase and went north. We got out there and the lieutenant was lost. He had no idea where the village was. I was so hard-headed I wasn't going to tell him. I just let him go ahead.

He lined up the platoon facing what used to be an old Korean compound. There was a fence there, but the old Korean firebase was gone and it was overgrown with vegetation. He lined up the third squad in the center, first squad on left and second squad on the right. He said he was going to go with the first squad to the left. Well, any leader knows you should be in the center of your command of any action where you can control movement and know what's going on. I figured if he's going to be over on the left, I'll stay here with the third squad. At the last minute, before he called in the illumination, he decides he's going to go with the third squad. I eased off without saying anything and went to the second squad. When the illumination popped all three squads started moving into the brush. The third squad had not gone 20 or 30 feet when they hit a 105-round booby trap. Americans dropped 105 rounds and they don't all explode. Charlie will get these rounds, stand them up and booby trap them because it's still a live round. When that squad went in there, it exploded.

It was a terribly loud explosion. I ran from about 75 yards or so away and was the first one there. The whole jungle was blown back clear in a round circle, about 60 or 70 feet in diameter. The guy right there as I went in was Sgt. Judy. He was sitting on his behind with his two legs up in the air in front, leaning back on his hands. One leg was blown off above the knee and the other blown off below the knee. Blood was shooting out his legs every time his heart beat. This illumination we'd fired from artillery was lighting it up just about like daylight. I got down on my knees in front of Sgt. Judy.

"Help the other guys. I'm OK," he told me.

Sgt. Judy was sitting there with his legs gone, knowing exactly what's going on. Some more guys started coming in and I told them to get tourniquets on him and stop the bleeding. I went to the next guy and I put guys on him to stop the bleeding. Two or three of the other guys was rolling around screaming in great agony. Three of the guys were dead already, but I got at least two guys on every man to stop the bleeding and give them drugs for pain.

I put out security on each end. Then I saw the once-cocky lieutenant lying on the ground, crying. I went to the radio operator and called for a dust off from Chu Lai, since the lieutenant couldn't. I needed two choppers for 11 guys, both KIA and WIA. they landed we loaded the first chopper up with bodies and it took off. The second chopper came in and we put bodies on it.

I remember two guys carrying this one fellow. We put the least injured on the first chopper and we put the dead on the second chopper. This one guy had his foot, still in his boot, but it was dragging along the ground while they were carrying him. It was only hanging on by his tendons. I picked his foot up and set it in the chopper with him when they put his body in. For years, and still sometimes, I wake up with that boot in my hand putting it in that chopper. That was one of my men that just a few minutes earlier was in perfect health.

While that dust off was coming in, up at the village we were supposed to hit, a Viet Cong was shooting small arm weapons toward us. It was ineffective fire from 600 yards away. We had everybody piece up all the gear we could find and we started moving back to LZ Stinson. We got down about 200 meters and by then with illumination coming in you could see the village silhouetted up there so you knew where it was then. I knew where it was all the time.

After we absorbed all that had happened, Lt. Billups said he wasn't going to let things stand as they were and started screaming like a wild man.

"We're going to kill everybody in that village and we're going to burn it!"

He started running toward the village. Several guys dropped their rucksacks and weapons they were carrying for the other guys and ran across a rice patty toward the village. I was screaming and hollering for them to stop, but they wouldn't.

I shot a magazine right over their head, so close I thought I might hit some of them. Half of them dove to the ground. The other half stopped.

"Just because we're stupid, we're not going to kill a bunch of women and children," I told them.

Lt. Billups still said they were going to the village. I locked and loaded another magazine.

"We're going back to Stinson."

The men started slowly, one or two at a time and then the rest went back to get the ruck sacks and weapons. We walked back halfway to LZ Stinson and we got into some elephant grass. I passed word to the back we were staying there until daylight. They just flopped down. As I walked back I made them get up and every other man face out and move out about five yards to the left and right. The rear man moved back up the trail a ways for rear security. We sat there from about 4 a.m. to daylight and I know not one man went to sleep. I heard some sniffling and crying. I let the lieutenant run a patrol and I was hard-headed enough not to stop him and let a bunch of my men get killed.

By the time we had daylight, we had plenty of time to sit there and think about what had happened. We moved around and went back up on LZ Stinson. Some of the men went to the battalion commander and complained about what happened. He called me up and asked me about it. I told him it could happen to anybody.

"Lieutenant said he was in charge. Didn't he want to run the patrol?" the battalion commander said.

"Yeah, he ran it, but it could have happened to anybody. It happens everywhere in Vietnam."

So of all my time in Vietnam, the one patrol where I lost my men was so terrible because I'd been used to winning. I hadn't lost anyone. Here, one of my last patrols, I'd lost a squad. Soon after that, the commander relieved the lieutenant and put him in a line company and we went to Happy Valley on a mission. We got word on the radio that Maj. Getz was sending out a shake-and-bake -- an E-6 who came into the Army and was real smart. They sent him to NCO school and made him a sergeant, then they sent him to Ranger school and when he finished, they made him an E-6. They sent him to Vietnam with about a year in the Army and made him a squad or platoon leader. They called them shake-and-bakes. This was going along with McNamara's 1,000, where they were getting troops anyway they could and making leaders overnight.

I was ordered back to the firebase by the battalion commander. I put the shake-and-bake in charge of recon platoon. He'd just gotten into the country and was in charge of a group of men in the jungle, fighting an enemy that was born in the jungle, born in war. The place where they overrun the firebase was Dien Bien Phu. That's when the French decided to pull out of South Vietnam. So this young E-6 with about a year in the Army was put in charge of 30 or 40 men in a jungle with the enemy with every man with at least 10 or 20 years of combat experience. I was brought back to the firebase.

"Tom, there's 27 drug heads on this firebase," Battalion commander said. "I want you to get them off of it and I don't care what you have to do to do it."

These drug heads refused to put on clothes. They refused to do their job. They refused to go to the field. They'd go into the chow hall and eat with no shirt on. Other NCOs and officers were afraid to correct them. They have a bunker off-limits to everyone else but them. It took me all of the next morning just to find all of these 27 guys and get them in one area where I was going to talk to them. They were wearing cloth shoes. Some were only wearing undershirts. They all pretty much told me the same thing: "You must be stupid if you think I'm going into the jungle and be the last American killed in your war."

They wouldn't let me talk. They asked if I was Super 7, a nickname of mine because we captured so many people and recon did so well.

"Well you ain't going to be Super 8," one threatened. "All you're going to do here is get yourself killed, because I don't play. I've been here three months and I ain't done anything and I ain't gonna do anything."

I finally got a word in.

"First thing here, you told a lie. You've been here three months and you haven't done anything? Well, you've been getting paid and you've been eating. Not one of you will go in that chow hall without a full uniform and a hat on your head straight, boots laced up and bloused and clean, with a haircut. If not, you won't eat anymore in that mess hall. And, you're going to get in that hole down there and fill 50 sandbags before you come out."

Sometimes I'd see them at the bottom of the hill with their hat cocked sideways until they'd get to the mess hall. I would tell them to walk back down the hill, get the hat straight and get back up before they could come in. I was making sure they were going to walk up that hill right and not just wait until they get close to me to put their hats on right and still think they were coming in.

Because I had to keep strict rules for these malcontents, I had to do it to everybody. This one line company had just come back from the field. I was at the mess hall door and these three good soldiers had been out in the jungle doing their jobs. They came in nasty, hungry and hadn't had a hot meal in three days. I told them they had to get a bath and get dressed properly before they went in. One of them pulled the bolt back on his weapon and chambered a round. He had his hand on the trigger as he took aim.

"You rear-echelon SOB. I'll kill you right now!" he yelled. "You're back here on the firebase and I'm in the jungle and you're going to tell me I can't come and eat?"

If his two buddies had not grabbed that boy, he would have emptied that magazine into my chest. When you have good soldiers out there doing a good job and then they come back in the rear and you start messing with them, you have a whole lot of trouble. They dragged him down the side of that hill. None of them came back to eat for that meal. For the evening meal, they came through the line and ate. When they were leaving I got one of his buddies and told him I appreciated them taking care of that boy.

"He would have killed you. He's still thinking about killing you."

"I know he would have killed me, even more than those drug-heads would have done it behind my back."

I told them I appreciated them doing a good job, but I was sorry, I have to do to them the same way I do the "problem children." That may have been the closest I came to getting killed in Vietnam -- by a good soldier that had just had enough of foolishness.

If you get into the Army and just slide by, you can still get along and get promoted. If you stand out and do what you're supposed to do, things like that are going to happen to you, because you're going to be the man out in their face and the other NCOs will be middling around behind you, letting you do the job. I was always the kind of guy who had to be the point man.

Later on, the drug-head soldiers all went down in the hole and about 10 of them just laid on the ground when they got there. Some of them filled their 50 sandbags and I told them where to be for guard duty. I brought the guys who wouldn't fill the sandbags straight to guard duty. That was OK with them. I put them on the first four bunkers. One man would pull an hour, then he'd wake up another guy. Then you had four guys to a position. When I put them out on the foxhole on the perimeter, some of them just laid down in the foxhole and covered up with the poncho to go to sleep while on guard duty.

I walked around the perimeter and they threatened to kill me. I came back and they were lying there asleep. I picked up a sandbag and dropped it on one of them. I walked to the other one. His weapon was laying up there. I took his weapon and fired a whole magazine right over his head. All night long I'd check them every two or three hours and I would pull havoc on them. I'd take their weapons and throw them back over a bunker somewhere where they wouldn't be able to find them. When you lost your weapon, you had to pay for it. They were complaining that I was hiding their weapons, but the colonel asked them how I got their weapons if they had them in hand while on guard duty.

Four days after being assigned to get the drug-heads off the fire-base, word came that my recon platooon had walked into an enemy Viet Cong bunker complex were four of my men were KIA, killed in action, and four were WIA, wounded in action. The Shake'n'Back who replaced me had the right side of his face blown off.

That morning I got my drug-heads together and never knew I could hate so deeply or want to kill so badly. "You said that you were going to kill me before returning to duty in the field. I am not responsible for your wellbeing. My re-con men are dead because I've had to babysit you trash. So please let me catch you asleep on guard duty and please try to kill me so that I can kill you and not go to jail."

While I was dealing with these drugheads, I was assigned as 1st. Sgt. of E Co. (NCO in charge of enlised personnel on the firebase). This one E6 named Alvarez decided that he didn't want to be in Vietnam or even in the Army at all, so he was assigned to me.

A few days later, I got up and walked by his area and saw tha the had laid all his equipment out for a full field inspection and was standing at attention, naked, and reporte dto me, "Sgt. Alvarez ready for inspection, sir." I told him to put his clothes on and stop playing around. I said, "You aren't crazy and when I get back, you'd better have your clothes on and your gear put up."

Thirty minutes later, a young soldier came to me and said, "Sgt. Bragg, you won't believe what Sgt. Alvarez did. He s--- on the VIP helicopter pad and he's still naked!"

This was the worst month and a half of my life. I had to hide to sleep, because they fully intended to kill me. I'd go to the artillery area and crawl into their bunker. The artillery had the largest ammo bunker on the firebase. It was about 60 feet long and about 12 to 15 feet deep. I would crawl on the ammo boxes as far back up in there of that 60 feet, with the spiders and the snakes and get a few hours sleep. Then I'd go back around the perimeter and wake these guys up or raise sand with them.

Some of them started volunteering to go back to their units about as soon as I lit a fire underneath them. Some of them said they weren't ever going back and I wasn't going to make them do their job. One night I left the perimeter around 11 p.m. I returned to the orderly bunker, where a first sergeant is supposed to sleep and they have a generator running all night with a light in the bunker. You also had a field phone in there.

When I walked up the hill to the CP Bunker, I saw a light shining out the door of the bunker. I got so close and on the side of the door in the shadows was a Claymore mine set up, facing out from the CP Bunker. I fell on the ground, rolled around to the side of the bunker. I was wet with sweat. I knew what a Claymore mine would do. It will cut your legs right off. That Claymore mine was sitting there waiting for me. I didn't stay there too long, but it felt like forever. I went around and I found a wire connected to it. A Claymore mine has a wire that goes down about 100 or 200 feet and it has a plastic clacker that you mash to blow it up. It just happened the clacker was lying there on three sandbags with nobody around.

About that time from the bunker line, a guy was talking with people down there, smoking a cigarette. He had gone down to bum a cigarette, which saved my life or saved my legs at the least. I squatted down. When he walked back up the hill toward the clacker and three sandbags, I started beating on him pretty good. The other guys started coming from all directions and got me off of him. He was arrested and sent back to the rear. A few nights later I was walking around through the bunkers on the firebase and there was a trail or place where people have all walked around these bunkers. It was around 3 a.m. and I started around that way. When I got about halfway, I decided to turn and go between these two bunkers which were just wide enough to get through. When I was going between them, a hand grenade went off where I would have been if I would have kept going straight. Again, my life was saved by fate.

A few days later, about mid-morning, I heard a boom box playing the "Pusher Man" song. This is a song that curses God over and over. I told them to turn it off and if I ever heard it again, I would demolish the boom box.

The owner said it was private property and that I couldn't take his property. "Turn it on and see," I said. I went and checked on other things and returned to hear the "Pusher Man" again.

The sound was coming from a bunker and before I got in the bunker someone passed it out a window (vent) and another man ran with the boom box. I then told the ownere that if I ever saw it again, even if it was turned off, I would destroy it.

You know, I never saw or heard it again.

After about a month and a half, almost all these guys had gone back to their units, the hospital or something. Only one of them was left. I had him down in a foxhole filling sandbags when I came to check on him. He said if it was the last thing he ever did, he was going to kill me. He was going to look me up back in the world and murder me. Amid his sandbag filling and threats, he fell over on the ground, weak as water. I picked him up and carried him to the aid tent. The captain said the guy had advanced stages of malaria and might die. They sent him back to the rear hospital and he survived. He came back in a month or so and had changed to become a good soldier.

After I got the drug heads on the firebase, Maj. Getz reminded me he had promised if I did a good job he would get me back in G Company Rangers. He gave me a pass to go anywhere in Vietnam as long as I wanted and then report to G Company Rangers in Chu Lai. I was a complete wreck physically and mentally because I had become an animal dealing with those trouble-makers. My Recon platoon was destroyed because I was dealing with misfits instead of doing my real job. They should have been out there doing their job. I didn't care if I killed them or if they killed me. Even the good NCOs and officers on the fire base shunned me as the strain turned me into something else. When they saw me coming they went the other way, just like they did with those drug heads. They thought I had gone completely crazy -- and I was crazier than the drug people. At least they thought I was because they got themselves off the firebase and went into the jungle to fight Charlie, rather than fight me.

I later left Chu Lai on a plane and landed in Saigon for a few days, then went to Da Nang to report to the G Company Rangers.

I hate to acknowledge how some soldiers react to conflict, but that's what happens in war. People actually rebel and they don't want to die. They're scared and they try to find someway to get out of doing what they're supposed to do. Whereas, if they did what they're supposed to do and everybody worked together, fewer people would be killed and they would be much more successful.

Chapter 7.5
Company G. 75th Ranger Regiment

I reported in at 1500 hours to G. Co. and went to their club. Sgt. Hammer and Sgt. Dickey came in and picked a fight for no reason. They were real tough guys.

We fought a while and I said, "Wait one minute. Let's get a beer. I'm tired."

We had a few and about 9:30, or 2100 hours, we were drunk. they said I was a pretty good dude, after all. They said a 1st lieutenant paid them $50.00 each to beat me up because I had flunked him on patrol back in Ranger school. When the old man (company commander) learned what the lieutenant did, he relieved him that day.

I was in charge of half of G Go. (or G-2) and we were to replace the Marine Force Recon on Freedom Hill west of DaNang.

Believe it of not, we had not one bit of trouble. Marines were like Rangers and the force recon was professional.

I spent my last two months on a hill protecting a battery of artillery (105). One day a chopper came in and the captain and colonel got off. I went down and reported. They said, "Sergeant, how many people do you have here to protect these guns?" I replied, "Nine men and myself, sir." He said, "You only have ten men to secure these four 105 guns?" I said, "Yes, sir."

The captain said, "Sir, these are Rangers."

The colonel said, "Oh, oh, okay," and they left.

After this assignment, I returned stateside.

CHAPTER 8 -- FROM RANGER TO RECRUITER

The war in Vietnam was winding down. Before it became a part of my past, I had to think of my future in the Army. Wherever I was going, I wanted to take success with me.

While in Vietnam, I volunteered to be an Army recruiter. They had already decided by 1971 they were going to make a volunteer Army because so many people were upset with the Army about their children being drafted and getting killed. When you get a lot of rich people upset about their sons being sent over to fight a war and after the war nothing's changed, it goes back to being the way it was before.

At that time, recruiting had priority on the assignment, so I got involved. Now an 11-B is an infantryman -- you expected them not to be too smart -- but an OOE is an administrative job. You'd expect one of them to be able to somewhat read and write. I came back from Vietnam and I got orders while on leave sending me back to Ranger department. I didn't want to go back to Ranger department. That order amended the initial orders I received sending me to recruiting school at Ft. Benjamin Harrison, Indiana. I said, heck, I got two more weeks of leave. I'm just going to go on to recruiting school and if Ranger department comes to get me, they'll have to come to Ft. Benjamin Harrison to get me.

Recruiting school wasn't difficult at all. I was assigned to Bartow, Florida in the Jacksonville District Recruiting Command. You'd get a guy, fill out a little paperwork on him and send him to the AFIS, either the one in Jacksonville or the one in Miami. When they got to AFIS, they would give them more tests and a physical and they would either allow them to go into service or reject them. They would also classify if that person was guaranteed a school, then they would set him up for basic training before the school.

There were already two recruiters in Bartow, so being the new guy they assigned me the worst recruiting area of the three, which was the town of Ft. Meade, Wauchula and Arcadia. Once a week I'd ride down to Arcadia to recruit.

Recruiting areas are broken down per number of people. Each recruiter has the same amount of population. Waycross, Georgia was the best recruiting area in America. Recruiters there were superstars because they made their mission by double. The reason was because in Waycross, as it was in much of South Georgia, there wasn't as many job opportunities. When a kid fell out of school or graduated, he would generally try to go somewhere else to work. Bartow was below Lakeland and between Tampa and Orlando, so there were jobs around them. Ft. Meade, Wauchula and Arcadia went all the way to Ft. Myers, but it was inland off the beaten trail from Tampa to Sarasota to Ft. Myers, so this was a country area where there was mainly orange groves and farming was about the only thing out there. I had no trouble reaching my objective. The biggest problem was finding guys who could pass the test and physical to get in.

It was really a special recruiting station because we were about halfway between Jacksonville and Miami and I would send them to Jacksonville and, say they flunked the physical, then I would take the same guy and a week later send him to Miami. That time he would pass the physical and flunk the test. Just the opposite in some cases! A lot of times they would go in, but after they took the physical and test they had to wait a year to do it again. Very few guys ever came back a year later and wanted to try again because they were doing something else by then.

Sgt. Gibbs was my station commander. I would get my objective every month, which was generally recruiting three to four people a month. I had no trouble getting mine, plus sometimes an extra person. I would give my extra to one of the other two recruiters because they were always one or two short. It was really terrible the pressure they put on recruiting. Vietnam was over, so there was an extra emphasis on making recruiting objectives. If you didn't, it was viewed as your area commander and deputy area commander didn't do their job and, along with the DRC (District Recruiting Command) commander, they had fallen short of expectations. Every man had to make his mission for everybody to be successful.

I was down there in a little place, Zalfo Springs, which was really a little town with one store at a crossing. I got this boy out of the swamp out there. He really wanted in the Army. They had been working him pulling poles out in the swamp. He was a big ol' rough guy. I called him that morning and met him at a store there. They were trying to get him on the truck to go back in the swamp and pull logs. He asked me if I would take him in the Army. I told him sure. Right there on the hood of the car I typed up his papers and waved down a Greyhound bus. The bus driver knew me because I was known for getting somebody, waiving a bus and sending them right on. This guy went to the Miami AFIS entrance station.

When I got back to Bartow, the station commander said someone wanted me on the phone. This doctor in Miami wanted me to call immediately. The doctor giving the physical told me to get down there immediately and do not stop until I got to the entrance station. He wouldn't tell me why, just that it was a direct order to be there within three hours. I hung up and called a guy I knew down there at the AFIS and asked him why the captain was calling.

200

"That idiot you sent down here has got Hepatitis C and it's highly contagious," my contact said. "We're restricted to the AFIS for the next five days. He wants you to come down here where you will have to stay in here with us for sending that boy down here."

There was another time when a guy came into the recruiting station and said he wanted to drive one of those big trucks that bent in the middle with the air brake (and described it by making the air brake sound effect) -- otherwise known as an 18-wheeler. So he joined a car load of recruits I was taking to Jacksonville. There was a big guy in the front seat, a little guy between me and him and another big guy in the back seat with two other guys. When we were coming back from Jacksonville, I asked which ones wanted to go home first, the ones at Ft. Meade or the ones at Bartow. Big boy in the back said, "Take me to Bartow first." The fellow in the front seat said, "It ain't Bartow, it's Bar-tow, so take me to Ft. Meade first."

"You hear me? I said Bartow. Take me to Bartow," the guy in the back replied.

"He doesn't even know where he lives. Take me to Ft. Meade!"

I told them I had to take them somewhere, but I didn't want any trouble. It made no difference to me since I had to go both ways. They insisted I stop the car. Diplomacy was out the window at this point.

They got outside and fought on the roadside. After a few minutes they got back in the car and decided they didn't care where they went, be it Bartow or Bar-tow. They had a bad dispute over how to pronounce it. Now I'm afraid I still don't know how to pronounce it.

When I got in recruiting, it was wonderful. They had a thermostat on the wall. You could make the temperature whatever you wanted, hot or cold. In Vietnam in the infantry, I never had a thermostat before. Then they gave me a government car with a credit card. I could not believe I was a sergeant in the Army and they were giving me all this stuff. Before, they just gave me my weapon and said go accomplish the mission. Now I had all kind of equipment.

I was in the recruiting station trying to figure out how to do stuff, looking in the file when the door opened and someone came in. I didn't look around at first, but when I did, it was Col. Dismuke. I didn't know Col. Dismuke. When I turned around and reported to him, he said, "You SOB, sit down." There was a pause as I speculated what was coming after such a greeting.

"You're down here really recruiting. I'm so glad I got you! You've been here two months and made your mission," he said, almost gleefully. "I wish I could get all these sorry son-of-a-guns to do their job."

Turns out, I had put the colonel through Ranger school, but I did not remember him. They called him "Jungle" Jim Dismuke. Col. Dismuke was one of those old-time hardcore Rangers. He lived it every day. Ranger this and Ranger that. The colonel didn't mind chewing a fellow out and talking bad.

About a year went by and I continued to make my mission. One end of the month came and our DRC fell way short of the mission, perhaps only around 70% of the goal. Our area had done the worst. We got a call in Jacksonville for every recruiter to report to headquarters in our district in Tampa by 1700 hours. Col. Dismuke had the sergeant major drive him to Tampa. He got there late.

We were lined up outside the building, going in one at a time. You have never heard the chewing out in the third degree as the colonel did. When it came my time, I was the first one from our station as I went in and reported to him. He was so upset he couldn't even talk to me.

"You just stand here Tom. I can't say anything to you because you have yours. You always do. Send in the next man."

The next recruiter in was from my station and he never made his mission, but the other recruiter and I got extra guys, so it would cover for him. Col. Dismuke started talking to him in a manner that, if it had been me, I would have hit the colonel upside the head because the colonel was just screaming at him to the point the recruiter was crying. I later drove this sergeant back to Bartow.

"If you had hit him or screamed back at him or something, he would have had more respect for you," I told him. "But once he talked to you that way and you just stood there and started crying, he had no respect for you."

That's how intense the volunteer Army was after Vietnam. They were determined the volunteer Army was going to work, but it never worked until they started paying soldiers a good salary and giving them good benefits. Some of the bonuses were $10,000 to $20,000 to re-enlist in certain jobs. I knew all the time you couldn't get high-quality people to stay in the Army when they could get more pay outside the Army and get a better job doing the same thing and stay in one place without a chance of being ordered to combat at any moment.

My time in Florida was very productive professionally and personally. I was in a church regularly by attending an Assembly of God church. I was there Sunday, Sunday night and Wednesday. I ran what they called the Royal Rangers, which is a group the Assembly of God church has like the Boys Scouts. Whoever wrote their handbook had been a Ranger in the Army. When I started my group in Bartow, I didn't have to read the manual. I knew it all. It was a miniature version of Ranger school for boys and men. Royal Rangers is an international organization. The Assembly of God church has a great number of Royal Ranger troupes. It's really an outstanding organization. The leaders have to pass the same requirements as the boys as far as building a fire, cooking a meal, preparing food, identifying different plants and doing community projects. I had 60 boys and men in the Royal Rangers, who met Wednesday nights. We would go camping four or five times a year and I would take them in the swamp or on the river and jamborees. We always won first-place prizes. We started meetings by playing different kind of games and then we'd go inside for a business meeting and plan what we were going to do.

My first birthday party there fell on a Wednesday night at First Assembly of God Church in Bartow. As I marched the Royal Rangers into the activity hall, I was the last one to come in. Everybody from the church had snuck into the activity hall. When I came in, they sang Happy Birthday to me and had some cake and a few gifts. I didn't even realize it then, but that December night in 1972 was my first birthday celebration. When your birthday comes right before Christmas, there's no need having a birthday because you're not going to get two sets of gifts, especially how I grew up. You're getting one or the other. So I had never really had a birthday party before then.

My last year or so in Florida I was in Plant City. They moved me in a trailer, but I was the only recruiter there in Plant City. I had no one to report to or no one to even talk to in my office. I just went to my trailer, headed up and down the road recruiting my area. Then I went to a church in Keysville, where I had a Royal Ranger troupe that was really big, with all country boys.

I remember riding down the road in Plant City when I saw a young man walking down the road from his roofing job. He had his roofing belt on, with a hammer, blue jeans and shirt ragged and a torn-up hat. I picked him up and asked about what he did. He said he couldn't do roofing anymore because they didn't want to pay him much. He didn't have a car to get to work and he was on bad luck. He asked if I would take him home. I rode north out of Plant City about six miles up to an old farm house, where vegetation had grown up around it. He was living there with his wife and they had just had a baby. They also had a German Shepard. I think they called that dog Kato. I still don't know if he was renting that house or if they just moved into it. It looked like it had been abandoned.

The guy told me he had three years prior service in the Army and he had been out about a year or so. He wanted to go back in and I wanted to help him. He gave me a 12-gauge shotgun with a long barrel that I still have today. I picked him up the next day to put him on the bus. On the way to the bus, he asked if I would keep his dog and if I could let his wife and baby stay at my house for about a month until her sister and her husband in Alabama could come down and pick them up. He also asked me if I could also take a few things he had, a bed and tables and such, and put it in storage for him. I responded I was a bit uneasy with taking all that on, but he insisted he couldn't go into the Army unless I did that for him because of his family.

"I got to get in the Army. I got to do something," he pleaded. "We're starving to death. We don't have anywhere to live and it's pitiful."

This was about 1974, when recession set in and a lot of people were out of work. You'd see a lot of people from up north -- car tags from Michigan, Ohio, New York, Pennsylvania -- riding around in station wagons with a mattress on top of their car and children inside. Some would set up camps out of town where they were trying to hold their family together. I felt bad about all those people, but in the Army I didn't get paid enough to help anyone with anything.

I put the guy on a bus to Jacksonville and went back to the office. The next day I learned he passed the test and physical and was going to Ft. Jackson. I drove to his house, picked up his wife, their child, the dog and a few belongings, and took them to my house.

Mind you, I hadn't told my wife we would have company for a month.

I went back and got this other fellow to help load the recruit's belongings in my truck so I could put them in storage at Lakeland. Just like he said, about a month later, his wife's sister and her husband came from Alabama and picked them up.

Eventually I was told I was on the E-8 list and that I couldn't stay an E-7 and remain a recruiter. I was going to have to go be a deputy area commander. Every recruiting area had a captain, an E-8, a deputy area commander along with station commanders. An area may consist of 20 or even 60 recruiters and four to seven recruiting stations. This captain from Washington called me after a while and said, "Don't you know somebody where you can go get a job? You've been in the Army long enough. Surely you know some people."

My principles hadn't changed since Vietnam.

"I thought you'd send me where the Army needed me."

"If we send you where we need you, it's the worst area in recruiting. They never make mission," he said. "If you go there, your career is shot and you'll probably be relieved of duty. You need to be calling somebody and find yourself a job where we won't have to send you there."

I told them to go ahead and send me there, because I had never backed down from a job yet.

These recruiters in Chicago were always used to regular soldiers. They weren't used to having a combat veteran, a LRP, Ranger and jungle expert. I called them together after I was there for a while to have a picnic, because in Chicago they have a lot of huge parks spread out around the suburbs. Everybody got out there with their wives and children. After a while we called them together so I could give them a little talk.

As I began speaking, I noticed everybody was trying to get my attention. There was a spider coming down out of the tree I was standing under. The spider kept easing down as I kept talking. I knew the spider was there, so I just opened my mouth, turned my head and lunged at him. I made out like I bit him, but he actually dropped to the ground. The wives starting saying I was an animal, eating spiders, and up there making their husband work day and night. They said I should be locked up somewhere instead of out in the public. That was an opinion a lot of people had of me even when I was a Ranger instructor.

A lot of Ranger students put on their after-action report that they knew I was caged up when there were no Ranger students there. When they showed up, they turned me loose on them. Any time a class graduates, they can write up anything about anybody or any phase of training or tactics. Every time I had about 20 students write up that I was sub-human or unbelievably crazy and should be locked up. I caused a lot of that stuff because I knew about those comments and I tried to act a little bit more crazy and wild to keep the reputation going.

Back then Rangers loved somebody like that. Over the years, some special units were organized from select troublemakers. They would go to prisons or go to units that were having lot of people getting in trouble. They would have those guys volunteer and go in units where they might not make it to commute the sentence or either they were facing court martial in the Army when they'd give them a choice of getting a court martial or going into the Ranger-type unit. In Vietnam, all them boys volunteered out of the 101st. We had everything from murderers to people who just wanted to have excitement, as well as the wild and weird people. We had all kinds in these special units I was in.

When time came, I'd left a week early and went to Chicago and checked the area out. I drove around in my Army recruiting car in the Addison area around all those little towns. I didn't talk to any recruiters, but I looked at the recruiting station and the area. I'd been told this was going to be a terrible assignment. I was fooling around on the road talking to some people and I ran into this kid who said he was thinking about going into the Army. I told him I was a recruiter, though I was in civilian clothes, and I could put him in the Army. He asked me to talk to his parents.

We rode through a middle-class neighborhood. I went into their home and spoke with his father, including breaking bread with them. After two or three hours, they signed for him to enter the Army. Naturally, I had all my paperwork with me. As a recruiter, you got to have your basic equipment with you at all times because you never know when you'd run into someone who wants to go. They may want to go right now and 30 minutes later they may not want to go. You can sell a man insurance or you sell a man on buying a car or house, but when you sell people on giving three years of their lives and committing to go through hard training and harsh conditions without knowing where they're going to be stationed -- and at a time when they didn't make much money -- you'd have to be called a great salesman.

I completed his paperwork and picked him up about two days later to take him to the AFIS in the loop of Chicago. You're talking about a Georgia boy in the loop of Chicago, with people that talk funny, and put a recruit in the Army in one of the Addison area recruiter's names.

I continued to fool around there for another week or so before my area commander, Capt. Murphy, was going to pick me up at the DRC. He was a West Point officer from the Midwest. He had three or four children, a good-looking wife and was as good of a man as you ever want to meet; the salt-of-the-earth kind. We were driving back from Ft. Sheridan on the far north of Chicago to the near westside of the city. He started telling me there had been a complete disaster. His career was going so good until he got into recruiting. He was not trained to lead a sales force. The captain actually started crying because he knew he was going to get a bad Officer Evaluation Report (OER). When you change command, leave one unit to the next, your commander has to write you an efficiency rating. There was no way his commander was going to be able to write him a good rating with not meeting the objective.

When he started crying, I held my hands out and told him he was in good hands, just like Allstate.

"Don't worry about anything. All you do is keep your door cracked so the recruiters know you're hearing what I'm telling them, so they don't turn around and try to tell you what I said, because I'm going to be hard. I'm not going to joke or play because this is serious business."

None of these nearly 50 recruiters had been in Vietnam. We'd had a war and they never left their hometown. They had been sitting there with a thermostat, a car with a credit card, living at home at night and talking with friends all day on the Army phone.

"It's going to be a little nasty, but I want them to know that you know what I'm telling them. I'm going to bring them in," I said. "Sir, we will do this thing. We have a big problem, but when we get there and I talk to these recruiters, you'll know what I'm talking about. I'm the bad guy and you are the good guy."

We got to the area headquarters where we had all the recruiters present -- except one. Believe it or not, this one recruiter would get up in the morning, go to the American Legion and drink beer all day. Everybody knew it. No one seemed to mind.

I went to find him at the office and was told he left around 10 a.m. When I found that sergeant, he lasted about a minute before he had his little behind going to the district headquarters to get himself shipped to Korea, first-class, immediately. He's lucky I didn't put my hands on him. He told me he wasn't a recruiter, so he didn't care and wasn't going to recruit. He'd been there a year and done nothing but leave his apartment and get drunk every day. I forget his name and I didn't want to remember his name, but nobody in that area (DRC) could be successful because he wasn't doing his job.

I got back and the captain and I had everybody else at headquarters. These men's uniforms were worn out. They hadn't bought new uniforms in years. Their boots, their shoes, low-quarters, were not shined at all. I'm sure some had cardboard in their shoes. The heels were worn down to the ground. Their hats were soiled and unserviceable. I walked into the room and looked around as the captain introduced me. The grapevine in recruiting is very strong, because these recruiters all have telephones and they all talk to one another. Most of the recruiters spent half their time on the telephone talking to friends or family. And these boys here knew about me.

They'd been told they were in a lot of trouble. There was a gorilla coming their way and he's not very smart. It got exaggerated as it came along, so by the time I got there these boys were ready for a shock. They needed it.

And I was ready to do just that as I addressed them.

"I am Sgt. Bragg. I have been in the Army 16 years. I have never been a failure. I have always accomplished my mission and I always will accomplish my mission. I don't claim to be smart and I don't claim to be good, but I'm a soldier in the United States Army. I'm an Airborne Ranger. If you can't do your job, it's my job to pick you up and carry you up the hill. If you can't recruit anybody, you call me and I'm going to go out there and recruit somebody for you. You will make your mission whether you're assigned one person a month or 10 people. You will find warm bodies to sign the papers to go in the Army. Otherwise, we're going to have a lot of trouble. Every

Saturday, if you don't make mission that month, for every Saturday that next month you're going to be here with me for remedial training. See I've had remedial training in my life, now I'm going to give you some remedial training -- and you ain't going to like it."

Then I layed out why things were in such sorry shape there.

"You have one problem. You're not proud of yourself. You're not proud of your uniform and you're not proud of America. You're not proud to be in the United States Army. That's the first thing and number one thing. When you do that, when you guys become proud to be a soldier that's when we will be successful."

I reached over and grabbed one of their ragged hats and threw it in the garbage can.

"Nobody will wear a hat like this as long as I'm your deputy area commander. That hat is worn out, unserviceable and filthy. Do you think I would look at your and your hat that's nasty and sign up to go into the Army and be like you? No. Nobody's going to be like you if you're not proud of yourself and if you're not clean. You're going to take a bath everyday. You'll use mouthwash and brush you teeth and if you got some cream, you'll put it on your hand to rub it on your face and ears where you won't have any chap because it's cold in Chicago. I've already found that out, because I'm chapping and I put a little oil on for that. I'm going to keep myself clean and you're going to keep yourself clean. Any questions?"

One of the station commanders stood up to rebut.

"You don't understand. They won't even let us in the high schools up here," the sergeant said. "You can't recruit anybody."

I decided now was the time to bring up what I had done a couple weeks earlier before I officially started there.

"Did you have a man go into the Army last week in your name, that you never saw? A fellow named Deroski?"

The sergeant said he had.

"Did you ever see him? No? But he went in Army in your name. You got an enlistment and didn't even know who he was. Fellas, he just said you can't recruit anybody in this area. I'm from South Georgia and you're from here. You talk like the people here. I don't. I got here last week and recruited that man and put him in that sergeant's name. Don't you ever tell me you can't recruit somebody up here in Chicago. If you have any trouble, you call me. I will meet you and we'll go recruit somebody. I want you to have good-looking clothes on. I want you to know everybody in your town. I want you to know the barber. I want you know the people in the bank and I want them to know you're proud to wear the United States Army uniform of an infantryman, of a recruiter."

I would spend much of that first month walking the streets in their area and letting those men watch me talk to people. I didn't go to one area where that recruiter and I did not find two or three people to give us their phone number and name because they were thinking about going into the military.

That month, we went 100% mission. We went 100% every month thereafter.

When Capt. Murphy left, he had a max efficiency rating. When Capt. Reames came in, he had me meet his wife and his dog. He was so happy. Everything was going well for about two months and the colonel called. Capt. Reams said the colonel wanted to talk to you. The colonel told me they were having trouble in Highland Park and that I was being reassigned tomorrow as deputy area commander there to get the place straight. I told Capt. Reames and he got back on the phone with the colonel and told him he could not do that. The colonel told him something else. Reams took that phone and threw it against the wall and jumped up in a natural fit. I told him he could keep this going here.

"It's not right for them to take you away from here," he ranted.

"They don't ever move people from one recruiting district to another. You're my man!"

He wasn't the only one who felt that way, apparently.

Before I went to Highland Park, I went to put my retirement paper in after 20 years in service. I went to the DRC and told Col. Morris I was going to get out of the service. The colonel told me not to leave the DRC headquarter building until he told me to leave. He called Gen. Goodson, the USAREC (United States Army Recruiting Command) commander of all recruiters. USAREC headquarters was also at Ft. Sheridan. So I hung around, talking operations and supply with clerks and everybody. Then I was told to report back to the headquarters to Col. Morris. I got there and Gen. Goodson caught me in the hallway.

"What do you mean you're going to retire?"

"Sir, I got 20 years in the Army. You can retire after 20 years."

"You can't retire after 20 years. You won't retire."

"Sir, I'm going to retire. You can't keep anybody after 20 years."

"You will stay in the Army until I leave recruiting command."

"Sir, they relieved MacArthur, but MacArthur was a four-star general. You can't keep me in the Army. They relieved a four-star general, why do you want to keep an E-8?"

He said again I would not leave, so I asked under what regulation would they keep me.

"The needs of the service," he said sternly. "You'll see you cannot retire."

I put my papers in anyway. Needless to say, my papers got lost. So I stayed about four years.

They had training at Ft. Benjamin Harrison, Indiana where all the area commanders and deputy area commanders would attend a three or four day course to brief them on recruiting, if they'd never been in it before. They would have 50 to 100 guys there. I told them

I wanted to go, since they had to send somebody from the DRC, so I could take a little R&R. I got down there and by next morning we were in the classroom. The captain got up and said we were waiting on the USAREC commander, Gen. Goodson. I'm sitting there looking at these guys, new to it all, when I've been in recruiting for seven or eight years.

Then everybody jumped to attention as Gen. Goodson came through the door and walked onto the stage. He introduced himself and the nature of the sales business. Then he spotted me.

"Wait a minute. Tom! Sgt. Bragg, stand up! I'm giving all of you a direct order to pick this man's brain and find out everything you can from him while you're here, day and night. Don't let him rest. This is one man that can recruit anybody, anytime, anywhere and make everybody he has under him successful."

That makes you feel good and gives you a big head, when you can't read or write and the general is talking about others trying to learn something from you.

Not only did we make 100% every month for the first three years in the area I was in, I got all of my recruiters a two-year associate's degree and those guys were proud to wear that uniform by the time I left. They would shine their shoes and belt buckles. They had the gig line straight. The gig line is where your pants zipper is lined up with your shirt and the belt buckle is right on that. They had their hats square on their head with a haircut. And, believe it or not, most of them had taken a bath every day.

I eventually went into the Recruiting Hall of Fame for the Chicago district recruiting area. I just about did what I wanted to do, when I wanted to do it, where I wanted to do it.

That is, until a new colonel and new sergeant major showed up. Both of them had been in the Army during Vietnam, but neither had gone to combat. They were out to prove something. They called me into their office, giving me orders about how to do it and telling me how I would conform to their policies. I told them I sure would -- because I was already 22 years in the service where they won't let me retire and now these two are going to come in and chew me out about not doing what they want, because I don't know what they want because they just got here.

That went on for about two months until I went by the DRC head-quarters and saw this E-8 walking around there looking like he was lost. I greeted him and he told me he was assigned to the Highland Park recruiting area as the deputy area commander. I said he was the man I'd been looking for. Somehow, he'd been assigned to my job. I put him in the Army recruiting car, carried him out to introduce him to all his recruiters and station commanders, then took him to my headquarters with the captain. Then I showed him where his desk was. I grabbed my little bit of stuff and went back to head-quarters. I told the colonel and sergeant major I was there to be assigned to a new position. They asked what was I talking about. "My replacement is out there. I don't have a job."

They assigned me to a GS-13 civilian. They had created this job for a civilian to analyze recruiting and the different people who were being recruited. He liked me very much. Matter of fact, he wore all kinds of loud clothing: scarves, red and pink, funny-looking hats and all kinds of funny shoes and britches. He said he "adored" me. I told him I'd been assigned to work for him, but he needed to stop that "adoring" stuff. I know this is a new Army, but I ain't that new.

A few weeks went by where I was going to different schools out-side the area demonstrating hand-to-hand and repelling. The civilian was downtown in Chicago when he called me.

"Tom, get down here to the loop. HUD was in town and HUD is who I work for. We have two of the biggest hotels in the loop."

I drove to the loop to find him. He took me to his room, which had a big high bed with a mirror on the ceiling and a fireplace in the room. He said the room was $13 a night. (Only $13 dollars!?)

He said he had something else to show me in the basement of the hotel. They had a whole floor of nothing but businesses with booths where they had people in line with bags and boxes. They would go to a booth, like Delta, and Delta would give them a shaving kit with toothpaste, razor blades, a mirror and everything you would need to go on a trip. You" go to the next booth, Procter & Gamble, and they'd give you a box of soap suds and bleach. You'd go to the next one and there was a knife company giving you a pocket knife with screw-drivers and things. I mean the whole floor was booths. You could get all the sodas, hot dogs and hamburgers you wanted. You just stayed in line going around that thing. Some people were dragging two or three suitcases full of supplies

I told the civilian I was going to stay at the hotel too, since I'm part of this organization working for him. So we went to the desk to get a room. The clerk told me it would be $280. I told them I was with HUD and the guy I worked for said I was with him. They said they didn't care who I was with. The discount was only for minorities. I said it looked like I was the minority there. I was the only white guy other than the guy at the desk. That's the truth. I went through the line and got me a box full of goodies. The event lasted for about a week. On the news, I saw this woman leaving the HUD thing with three luggage racks full of boxes of things to go home. To see that stuff first hand, it's sort of shocking when you've served in the Army with people of all races, then to get in the civilian world and see certain people get special rates on rooms. But you still live in the greatest country in the world, even with all our problems.

At Ft. Sheridan, the headquarters for recruiting and a few other units in the midwest, I lived on sergeant major's row. My last six months, my kids got a job cleaning the offices at the base. They were

14 and 15 and they got a job cleaning these offices through the cleaning people, but they had to have an adult with them. So for them to be able to work, I would sit with them in the evening while they cleaned these two or three offices. I finally said, heck, I'm not going to sit here, I'm going to help them clean.

We would have a reputation in a few weeks of cleaning our offices better than other people. We were asked to take on the post headquarters, which had a basement and three more stories. My kids jumped on it because it was a full eight-hour building. You got paid a whole day's pay to clean that three-story building with a basement. I would help them as we started in the top floor dumping ashtrays, dusting off desks, dumping garbage cans, mopping the floor, cleaning the bathrooms. Then we'd go to the second floor, then back down to the basement. We would drag big plastic bags that were full. The plastic bag would be nearly as big as a car when we got to the bottom going out to the dumpster. I would roll that big bag full of one-night's cleaning into the dumpster.

Around that time, my wife decided she was going to go to Florida where we had a house that we were supposedly renting to another family. The people went to church with us and they had four or five children. We let them rent for just about nothing because they were really supposed to take care of the house. Well, they did neither. They didn't tend to it and they didn't pay rent for the house they left in a mess. So my wife and daughter left and went to Florida to get ready to retire and my son got another job. He didn't want to clean the building anymore because the kids at school started calling him a janitor. He quit and it left me cleaning the post headquarters by myself. Like I said, my replacement had arrived but I still had a few months to go in the Army.

When cleaning the post headquarters, I would run through the building cleaning it. I could mop a 100-foot hallway in less than a minute and a half. Some secretaries were working late one night and they saw the way I was running and cleaning the bathrooms and dumping garbage cans and pulling that big bag of garbage. So after a few nights, I started getting 20 or 30 people each night to watch me clean the building because I was jumping over desks and such. If it wasn't for my kids getting that cleaning job, I would have never got into that.

I had a job with Brown and Ferris picking up garbage first thing in the morning. The garbage route was so terrible. They put me with this man who was running the route already. In the wintertime, the water and everything is frozen in the garbage cans. I would run along the road grabbing bags and dumping garbage cans. I got the job because the man that ran the district for the company had his office down the hall from where my area recruiting office was. He had four or five secretaries there and I played golf with him a few times. He told me they were paying $10 an hour, back in 1978, so I got a job picking up garbage. But I ran the route so well, I would just drag the whole garbage can out there and dump it all in the back of the dumpster and pull the lever on the truck to compact it. The route had 80% complaints because it was cold, bad weather and the guys working there had slacked off. When I started running the route, the complaints went down to two or three a day.

I'd get up at 5 a.m. to run the garbage route and I'd finish by 11 a.m. Then I'd get a bath and put my uniform on and go through operations where I was supposed to work with the GS-13 with that HUD deal. I had no responsibility other than to check in. I'd then go back home and put on my janitor outfit and clean the post headquarters, which was an eight-hour building, until about 10 or 11 o'clock at night. In essence, for my last eight months in the Army, I was on the clock 24 hours day.

With the garbage route, the bossman asked me to stay on and he was going to give me a route where I just drove a truck and dumped the dumpsters without having to get out of the truck. But I had that house in Florida and I'd been down there recruiting, so I was heading back there.

I put my son on an airplane one day at O'Hara Air Base to fly to Florida and I was going to stay and finish clearing base at Ft. Sheridan and get discharged. When I put him on that plane, I stood up there at O'Hara Air Base and watched it fly off. My wife and daughter had already gone to Florida. It didn't hit me until my son left -- I was getting a divorce at the time -- that my family was gone. I started crying uncontrollably in the airport. Big bad Ranger, recruiter extraordinaire and leader, but it was all for not. King Solomon said it's all vanity and all goes with the wind. You can do anything you want to on this earth and accumulate homes, cars and money, but when you lay down there, there's nothing but you when you go out of this world.

After this short time, I put in for and got my retirement. I left Chicago in an old pickup truck. They did have a parade for me and a ceremony where they pinned the Army commendation on me and a few other medals. I cleared my house on the base. When you leave, they give you a white-glove inspection. Everything has to be perfect. It took me three days to clean that thing. I scrubbed and scrubbed and it still didn't satisfy them. I drove back to Florida where I had a house I had been renting out. Problem was, the people there hadn't paid rent. They just lived there while I was gone.

For the second time in my life, my financial rug had been pulled out from underneath me. I was scared to death. But it was the first time in my life without Uncle Sam backing me up. I had a little retirement check, but no skills other than I knew how to run up a hill with a gun in my hand.

CHAPTER 9 -- THE LONG TRAIN RIDE HOME

When one door closes another one is supposed to open. Sometimes it takes time to find it, though.

I had left the base in Chicago in an old pickup truck headed to Columbus and still uncertain about my future. I was 41 years old and I had a house there that those people had lived in and run down. Sitting in the yard was a two- or three-year-old Lincoln Continental without a drop of oil in it, surrounded by grass growing up to the windows. The house was half-finished, but I had the name of a carpenter who I called to come back and put the toilets in since he had been paid to do it. He said he wouldn't come back down there for any kind of money.

Here I was with my son, going to school, and with Robby, a good kid without much potential who needed a place to live since he had been thrown out of the Navy. One reason he got thrown out of the Navy happened when Robby was at the Great Lakes Naval Training Center just north of Ft. Sheridan, near Waukegan. He was working on his car in the parking lot when he accidentally set it on fire. The blaze burned up his car and the two cars next to his. Lo and behold he went back downtown and somebody sold him another car. So everyday when you'd go to work you'd see Robby's car by itself and nobody parked within four parking spaces around his car because they were afraid he was going to burn up their cars.

I got my son, Thomas A. Bragg Jr., enrolled in Plant City High School and I took Robby over to Bradley Junction. Well, the railroad had a track crew over there. I'd maxed the PT (physical training) test the last five years in the Army. I was in good physical shape at 40 years old as you could get. I could pick up a crosstie and carry it a mile. The only issue was the heart attack I'd had. At Bradley Junction, we asked to speak to the foreman about applying for a job laying track. The man asked me how old I was. I told him and that I was just out of the Army. He told me I was too old to be on a track crew, but he asked about Robby. I said Robby was a young man and could do it. He said he was red-headed, left-handed and I bet you he's Polish. The man said he's got three strikes before he starts. You might as well get out of here. So that's how we started out looking for jobs.

I went back to my church I had gone to at Keysville and a fellow who attended there was a subcontractor. One day he asked me if I would come work on a house he was building. He needed my help framing. I told him I'd never done it before and that I didn't know anything about carpentry, other than how to drive a nail. I told him Robby needed a job, so he told both of us to report to the house at 7 a.m. and he'd get us started. When we arrived, we saw there was just a foundation there. He told me where to put the walls and we started building the frame. There was another guy there working and we were told he'd been a carpenter for 10 years and would be in charge.

The next day when Robby and I started working at 7 a.m., this guy didn't show up and neither did the boss. About 9:30 a.m. here came this guy, who's supposed to be a carpenter, with a string of fish. On the way in he saw that pit and stopped to catch those fish and now he had to clean them. I asked about the work on the house. He said we didn't have to worry about it because the boss wasn't there that day. Within a week, the man had put me in charge of building the house, so I did it with Robby. We put up all the walls and then we put up the trusses. The electricians and plumbers did their things and they gave me pointers on what to do.

The man we were building the house for asked me if I would change something in the kitchen. I told him sure. When the subcontractor came out, I told him what the man wanted me to do and he told me not to do it. I told him it wouldn't be any trouble. He said don't do it no matter what he wants. I was caught between the guy I'm working for and the man we're building the house for, who came back with his wife mad at me. I said the subcontractor told me not to do it. He said he was the one paying and he wanted it done.

Robby and I put the roof on the house. Every time I saw that man for years after that, he complained to me about how bad that house was built. He'd see me and he'd sure carry on about it. I said,

"Well, I told you I wasn't a builder, but I did the best I could with that other boy hunting and fishing on the way to work and Robby was doing his best."

After that first house, I got a job at the Polk County Jail. Most everybody who gets a job at the jail is a correctional officer. They would hire just about anybody to do it so I got that job within the first month or so. I had a uniform and white shirt and they put me in there to put people in jail and lock the door. Robby kept working with the subcontractor.

After about a week or two, TAB had come from school. We were out in the barn and here came Robby, who had gotten him a little ol' car. The man he was working for used Robby's car to haul tools and paint. I had told Robby if that man was going to use his car as a company car, he should pay Robby extra for using it. Robby said he didn't want to say anything because he messed up a lot on the job.

Robby was flying down the long driveway, with dust going every whichaway. He wheeled around the house in the backyard, jumped out the car and ran over to the barn and every time his foot hit the ground he left a big spot of yellow paint. He was mad and cutting up.

He had a five-gallon bucket of paint sitting between the seats when someone pulled out in front of him and the whole five gallons of paint spilled down his console and filled up the floorboard.So when he got out, his shoes were full of paint all the way up the side of his ankles. We looked in the car and all that paint was all over the seats – and he had just got the car and loved it. I told him we might could fix it.

We got out there with a water hose and started washing the seats and floorboard and washed all that paint out of the car for Robby. By the time he got in the house we had filled that car up with water and then later vacuumed it with a shop-vac. I'll never forget Robby coming down that road with his red hair, blue car and yellow paint. I used to ask how a boy with blue eyes and red hair have yellow feet. He didn't think it was funny. It was always something like that with Robby.

At one point I'd planned to go in the cattle business and get rich. So I had a few cows out there. My cow had a calf that was a bull. Well we were going to fatten that bull up. It wasn't more than one or two years before he got big and healthy. I would get in the pen and hold his horns and he would snort and try to push me around. We had him locked up and was going to slaughter him. We were feeding him all the corn he wanted to eat to get him fat and take him to get him fixed up and put him in the freezer. My son was at a part-time job at the phosphate mine, so he had a bunch of his buddies come by. They were drinking beer and all when I got home.

"Show them how strong you are daddy," he said. "You can hold that bull."

Well that bull had already picked up 300 or 400 more pounds. I didn't want to, but he kept on about how I could do it. I decided to show off a bit. I got in there and grabbed the bull by the horns and immediately he charged me and my back hit the wall of the pen.

"Grab his tail, because he's about to kill me!" I told them.

I kept my arms straight, but that bull had picked up some weight. They grow fast, so I don't show off too much with that bull. I got out of that pen with a narrow escape.

With my job as a correction officer, all the rest of the guys who got that job did it for a while and then moved into being policemen. That was a stepping stone along with taking courses to get on with the city or county. I didn't want to be a policeman. I just wanted a job and everything was going well. One day I was up on the third floor, where the worst inmates were kept. When I was coming out the elevators I saw three or four correctional officers with this one big guy who would not go in his cell. They were trying to grab and hold him and he was kicking and punching them. As a correction officer, you can't hurt the prisoners. You're supposed to subdue them, but the prisoner will hit you upside the head. When I saw the struggle, I just ran up over the top and hit him right in the jaw, knocking him down against the wall. He tried to get up and one of the officers grabbed his arm and another grabbed the other arm and one on his head.

I grabbed his toe. His big toe, that is.

He was about 6'5" and had big, long toe. I was sitting on his back, pulling on his toe, so I had his leg twisted in an odd position where I was straining the ligaments. I pulled back on that toe and he would slide three or four feet.

"My toe! Oh, my toe!" he yelped.

I told the other officers they could turn him loose, because I had him. Along each side were jail cells with about four to 15 prisoners each. When I was right there between the cells and I'd pull his toe and he'd slide a ways. The guys in the cell were commentating.

"He's got Leroy by the toe. I've never see a toe hold before. That man has him, sitting on his back, riding him. Look at that. That's something else? Man, where did you learn that toe hold?"

When I pulled back again, the inmate said he would go in the cell if I turned his toe loose. I asked him once more, sitting on his back, before I let go of his toe. He promised he'd go to the cell. I told him I would do it one more time to make sure and he slid down on his arms, trying to crawl like a turtle. I let go and told him if he didn't comply, I'd do it again. The guy got up and hobbled into his cell and reached back and closed to door. All those guys in jail were laughing, having a good time making a big show out of the thing.

"I ain't ever seen a man lock himself up," one inmate said. "That toe hold was bad!"

The rest of the time I worked at the jail, anytime I came around there was somebody asking me where I learned to do that. I'd been doing hand-to-hand for more than 20 years, so I was well-equipped to know the weak points of the body.

Some people in jail are the lowest class people. Those who have never been in jail don't know how sorry and low-down the lowest parts of the community are. There are people that have no morals, no responsibilities and they care about nobody but themselves. They don't care if they go to jail or who they hurt. The only thing they care about is themselves at that moment. I'd been in the Army more than two decades and I thought I had served with every animal possible on God's green earth. I'd served with some fine men and some slackers. But this jail experience? I was introduced to another low of humanity. You couldn't understand them.

I was telling this one guy getting out of jail that this was an opportunity to straighten out, get a job, go to school and get a family. That didn't motivate him a bit.

"I'll knock a fool like you in the head and take your money. I'm not about to get a job. I'll get you if I see you."

I told him he'd be back in jail by next week. Sure enough, it was like a revolving door at times. Some would tell you they're not stupid enough to work for somebody, because they would take what they want.

I was giving out the mail one time when I went down to a cell with about 15 guys in the block. One inmate came to me and said if he didn't get a letter that day, he was going to hang himself. I called out the mail and he didn't have one. He went back to his bunk and got a sheet, tied it around his neck, climbed up the bars and tied the sheet high on the bar and hung himself. I'm standing outside with no key to the cell and the other guys in the cell are all standing back watching him hang himself. They thought this was good entertainment. The shortest guy in there was trying to hold the guy's feet up to save him, but he was kicking his feet so he couldn't hold him up. Then he started turning blue. The guys in the cell were saying we needed to do something.

I ran all the way up the hall to the office, got a key to the cell, ran back and opened the cell and got him down and outside the cellblock. He was just about dead, blue and barely breathing. I let him lay there a while and got the others locked up, with letters scattered all over the floor. I dragged this guy to the office and laid him up against the wall. He was really in bad shape. The sergeant of the shift arrived. I told him what the inmate did and what I did. Even after I later got a job on the railroad, I had to go back to court for this incident because someone claimed I "let" the guy hang himself. The judge asked me why I let him do that. I thought I was back in the Army, like when the colonel asked me why my men went to town and beat some people up while I'm at home in bed with my family. Now this judge is asking me how this idiot hanged himself and I didn't stop him.

"The only reason he's alive is because I got there just in time," I said.

I also had to go back to court for hitting that other fellow. He got himself a lawyer, but he didn't put in there that I had him by his toe.

One night I was on duty and the police pulled into the garage and closed it, so the troublemakers could get out the car and into our custody. A police officer told me he had one who thought he was bad and we need to be careful because he would try to hit us. This other boy and I went over there and opened the door. This average-sized fellow came out cussing and banging his head against the door, talking about how he was going to sue the world and whip everybody. I grabbed him and snatched him out of the backseat of that car down on the ground.

"You're not suing anyone while you're lying on the ground."

I drug him in there and got him to the desk. He wanted to be hateful. He wouldn't answer questions or take things out of his pocket or take his belt off. The woman motioned for me to put him in the holding cell. We got him in the cell and closed the door. He ran up there in that holding cell -- there's nothing but vents on each side and a little 6"x6" glass you can look in to see what they're doing. I looked in and he was banging his head on that little glass trying to break it with his head. His head was bleeding, after he was beating it against the police car. He was talking about what he was going to do to me if I would open the door and let him get to me. I left him in there for an hour or two and they said to check to see if he's calm and sobered up. He had been in an apartment complex trying to get in his girlfriend's apartment -- and he was married at the time. I told him to behave and later booked him and put him in jail.

Fortunately, I had a break coming.

The railroad called and said they had a time to interview applicants in Tampa. Now this was 1980, when we had a recession going on. There weren't many jobs and you'd see people from other states on their car tags. They set up hobo camps. These were people who were making $80,000 a year and it just collapsed. Here they were used to living the American dream and all of a sudden they have nothing.

At the railroad, there were lines there a block long going inside. When I went in, the man asked if I was an Army recruiter and sergeant. He pointed out how I was used to sitting on the other side of the desk. It sure felt funny sitting on this new side asking for a job. I was so used to all my jobs in the Army, not civilian life. He told me he was sending me for a physical that I had to pass. That worried me because I knew I had my broke disk and my cracked right hip. They X-rayed me and after they read it, they called me back to X-ray again. A woman there wouldn't tell me why. They did it again and I thought I was through. If there's one thing railroad doesn't do, it's hire people with a broke back because there's nothing level and it's easy to get hurt and they don't want to get sued.

They called 20 of us back for an interview. He didn't ask me about a broke back, just a few things about my work and qualifications. Lo and behold, they called me to work for the railroad. Another miracle. I got in the Army and couldn't read and I got into the railroad with a broke back. Do you think the good Lord is looking after Tommy? Unbelievable. Why? I don't know. They knew I had a broke back, but they still gave me a job.

There were about 10 of us they took into the classroom for a day or two to learn more about the railroad. Most of the guys in the group were young and had had a few jobs. We called each other Bubba, because I was so stupid I couldn't remember anybody's name. I would call them Bubba 1, Bubba 2 and Bubba 3. They said they were going to send us to Waycross, Georgia for a week of training: learn how to throw switches, couple up cars, cut in the air hoses and safety procedures.

I was out looking at my truck before I left for training, trying to put some water in the battery. I had a flashlight to help me see the water level. When my son turned around to look at something, the water hose splashed battery acid on my eyes. I washed out what I could, but my right eye was blurry and I couldn't see very well. When I washed my eyes out, I could see for about an hour, then it would get worse and cloudy. This was Friday and I was supposed to be in Waycross Monday morning. I drove, trying to save money, that Saturday morning to MacDill Air Force Base on the other side of Tampa to go into the hospital there. After checking my eyes, they told me I had to go to the specialist back in Bartow, Florida. They washed out my eyes and I could see better. I was driving blind, actually, on the way to MacDill. I got back home and the next day I went to a specialist in Bartow. He told me I had the equivalent of a bee sting on the pupil of my right eye. The battery acid had burned my right eye and my left wasn't much better. He told me to put two drops of this and one drop of that. Three kids of medicine. He told me if I didn't do all three, I'd be in great pain. He said I had to stay home and have no activity, because I may still end up blind. I told him I had to go to Waycross Monday. He said I was going at my own risk, but I had to have the job.

I went home and put the medicine in my eyes. I got with the Bubbas that Sunday evening and we checked into the Ware Hotel in Waycross. I didn't do anything but eat and put the drops in my eye. As long as I did that I could see OK, but I went through that week in Waycross half blind with those drops in my eyes. I went back and they put me on the railroad as a brakeman. That was one big thing in my life: getting in the Army, becoming a paratrooper, becoming a Ranger, then being a Ranger instructor and excelling at recruiting and, now, I'm a brakeman for Seaboard Railroad. I knew then I had fulfilled more expectations in my life than I ever thought I would from where I started. Here I was with what I considered a real good job, working outside in the elements, riding up and down the railroad track.

I was working there about four months and I got called to report to Lakeland, Florida to the yard office. They'd had a bad derailment in a place called Homeland, south of Bartow. When I got to Lakeland around 2 a.m., the engineer and I were there, but the conductor and flagman were not. He told me they lived in Orlando and on the railroad they were supposed to give you an hour and a half call, but on an emergency to go out with a work train, they would tell you to get there as fast as you could. These other guys had to drive from Orlando and they weren't there.

Then some men came in with a black tie and white shirt and they asked the engineer if we were ready to go. He said the conductor and flagman were not there yet. They told us to hook on the work train and cars and they were going to pull out. He said they could catch up when they arrived. We coupled up to about 10 cars, with a mess car and a crane chained down on a flatbed car, and then cars with rail and cross ties all chained. They keep this work train outfitted just for derailments. I told him I would just ride in the back of the train in the work car. I thought the door was open on that work car, but the last one had the door locked, so I rode on the outside for about 15 miles.

We got down to the big derailment in Homeland. I went around and all these workers came by the cars and they're standing around outside on the banks, near the rail. The engineer told me we had to switch out and put the crane in front of the engine and push it forward down to the derailment. That way the crane would be the first car on the train to pick up the boxcars and cross ties, clean up the mess and put the tracks down. I didn't know anyone there and had just met the engineer that morning.

These track workers were along the side of the train on these big banks on each side. We got the train switched around in the right order and these guys are just standing around. When I started to switch out, I had told them to get inside the car or get up on the bank because they knew this stuff could fall off the car. I was hollering and jumping on these guys. I'd only been there four months with no seniority. The sergeant came out in me and I took charge. The conductor and the flagman still hadn't got there. Then I went up to the front with the crane on the flatbed. Officials were standing up there just talking. I didn't realize who they were and I didn't care. The engineer was ready to go.

"You put your hands on something, because when this thing starts moving you could fall and kill yourself. I don't want to get anyone killed while I'm in charge of this train. Y'all grab something and don't turn it loose until I tell you!" I told them.

Then I had the train go forward and had to cross a dirt road and we had that crane in front of the engine. So I eased and the engineer followed with the train so we could see well up and down the dirt road and make sure it was clear before I told him to proceed and come ahead.

We got down to the derailment and I started giving orders to the crane operator.

"Get up on the crane. You boys undo the chain over there..."

Then one of the company officials came over and settled me down.

"You're not in charge here," he reminded me. "You're through for the day. You've done your job. Go back up yonder and they'll get you a ride back home."

I was going to pick up the derailment and relay the track if they would have let me. That's the training of being an NCO, Airborne and Ranger and taking charge of the situation and getting it done.

About a month later I got a call and the railroad asked me if I wanted to be a locomotive engineer. They had a class starting in about a month. The difference between a trainman and an engineer is different unions. With the engineer union, they can't lay you off. If they do, they have to pay you. But with a trainman and other workers on the railroad, they can tell them to go home and not pay them. Then they may be off a week or two or a year before they call them back. The engineer was the highest paying job on the crew and the most desirable.

The engineer is responsible for reading train orders and if you have any work orders along the way. You have to know the mile posts and know the tracks. If the slack on the train is going out and you're pulling the engine, you'll bust the train in two, because those knuckles will break. You can pull a complete draw head out. The knuckle is just the piece that couples together, but the draw head is that whole iron arm that goes under the car. Most people on the railroad will be hired at one depot and they'll work that line for 30 or 40 years, running the same track over and over. They know it so well that they know every curve and crack in the rail, but they moved me to every depot in Florida.

I worked in Tampa city yard as a hostler. A hostler is a young engineer who moves the engines around the yard. He takes them off an incoming train, takes them to a shop, fuel, clean and service them and then take them back out and put them on the new train being built. I worked Rockport, loading ships, mainly with phosphate because south central Florida had phosphate mines everywhere until they found out most all other countries had phosphate in the ground too. Then they started moving overseas.

I worked the sugarcane switcher in Clewiston for three months. I got to work at 6 o'clock at night and might get off at 10 or 11 in the morning. I'd run the empty racks out to the field and pick up the loaded sugarcane racks and back them into the sugar mill. That was a good job. The only thing was you had to live in Clewiston, where you're always away from home.

I worked the Miami switcher for a few weeks and lived right off the beach in Miami. That was just before they forced me to Jacksonville. That's when I saw the old turntable. In the old 1800s, they had a turntable where you run an engine up on this wheel-like platform. It would turn to another track any of the 360 degrees and you had a track heading off of that circle about every 10 or 15 degrees. If you wanted a certain engine, you'd line the turntable's track to line up with the engine's tracks. You'd get the engine on the roundtable and it turned to put you on the main track going out. It was fascinating to me how they stored all these engines in one place where they would work on them, too.

Then they forced us to Waycross. Same thing. They had too many engineers, business was down and they wanted some of us young engineers to quit. Waycross is quite a ways from Tampa. They had 15 qualified engineers with more seniority than us. They paid them to sit at home while we had to drive all the way from Tampa to Waycross to work their jobs -- all to try and make us quit. You know how many quit? None.

We drove our cars up there and tried to hang on to a job, because a railroad job for a country boy was mighty fine. I got to where my pay was about $100 a day. I thought that was unbelievable. All of the bills I had, all of the cars I bought, the land I owed for, I paid them off. I didn't miss any work for about four years.

One day I thought about my house in Keysville. I had worked all night and when I got off, I went over to the depot in downtown Wayross and called Jacksonville on their railroad phone to speak to the man in charge of forcing me to work in Waycross. I had a house and cows in south Florida. I told him he was going to tell me whether I'm going to stay in Waycross or if I'm going to be released to go back to Tampa. He said he couldn't tell me because they didn't know where they would need me. He said he would, however, give me $10,000 to go to Augusta and run the train there.

"Wait a minute. Augusta is another 300 miles away from my house," I told him. "That's twice as far."

He said that was all he could do for me.

For a man that can't read well and a man that can't run a train long enough to learn that route, there I was now going to go to Augusta, where they ran the train mainly back to Atlanta. I asked that man how late would they be open and he said I could come down tomorrow to sign the papers. I told him I'd be down there that same day. That was about 10 a.m. when I left for Jacksonville to go to the "Purple Palace." (They had merged Seaboard with Coastline and come up with the CSX railroad.) I went into that big building up to the fifth floor and found that man. I told him I wanted my $10,000 to go to Augusta. I went back to Waycross, spent the night and went to Augusta the next morning.

They put me in a hotel in the middle of downtown Augusta. I was doing firing, which I'd done around Tampa and Lakeland. All you do when you're firing is sit on the engine and watch the engineer run the train. These are routes you ride two or three times, so you're there making $100 a day looking out the window. That was some good training. I couldn't believe it. In the Army, they'd send you to get shot at and they wouldn't pay you much. (And you better not complain about it.)

So we ran the train to Atlanta and, could you believe it, we got to run by big Stone Mountain. We ran right into Atlanta, right in the middle of the city to Underground Atlanta where the train would actually go under the Omni downtown. When you came out the west side of Atlanta, you'd go to what they called "The Slide." If you got over six miles per hour on The Slide, you had a runaway train because it was so steep. At the bottom of the hill was Tilford Yard. As you come down the hill, the tracks would start going out in every direction. If your train was going too fast down that steep incline, the brakeman had to run fast so he could try to throw the switch and get you on the right track. I never will forget The Slide or going under the Omni.

I got into Atlanta and they called me to go on a coal train around to Milledgeville. I think it's Plant Vogle where they use all that coal. You ride the coal train all the way through Milledgeville and you back another 15 miles into Plant Vogle. When you get there, they take you off the engine and they carry you to the hotel to get eight hours sleep. You actually get six hours of sleep. When they call you, you have an hour and a half to eat and take a bath before getting on the train to go back to Atlanta. Then you hope you get a call to go back to Augusta instead of Milledgeville. Some guys spent a month up there in Atlanta catching the coal train to Milledgeville rather than going back home where their family was in Augusta.

They also sent me to run the Athens switcher. I'd been there about a month doing that and it was going pretty good. One day I was called to go to Atlanta and when I got there, I went to get by the window to watch the engineer run the train. It was about five in the afternoon and this ugly engineer came out there, scowling at me.

"What you doing sitting over there?" he grumbled.

I told him I was in the spot where the fireman sits.

"No, the fireman on this train sits over there," he said, pointing to the controls. "You're going to run this train. I'm going to sleep."

I told him I'd never run a train before. He asked how old I was and said he knew I'd been on the railroad a while. I told him that I wasn't long out the Army. It didn't matter. He told me I was going to run the train anyway. So, we pulled out of the yard in Augusta.

When you come out of there, you go about 10 to 15 miles up the side of a huge hill. You have to hope you have enough horsepower to get up that hill. I got up the hill and started toward Atlanta, where between Augusta and Atlanta it's ravines. It's not like the flat land of Florida or South Georgia. Up there, you're going uphill or downhill all the time. By the time you get the engine downhill, the back of the train is still going uphill and by the time you get the engine going uphill, the back of the train has decided to go downhill, so you have slack running in and out all the time. We got through Thomson and the engineer was asleep on a broken-open cardboard box while I'm running through these towns. I didn't know where I was at, but I was running the train.

It got to be around 9 or 10 o'clock at night when we pulled into Atlanta, going under the Omni and slowing down as we went down The Slide. I would ease up as I came down The Slide and the man threw the switch and we ran into the proper track. When the car came to pick us up to take us to the yard office, the engineer looked at me and said, "You're one hell of an engineer. You know your stuff." I asked how he knew that since he was alseep. He said he could tell I was good.

We got to the hotel room and moments later he came beating on my door. I was already tired and beat from paying attention to run that train. Well he kept beating on my door. I didn't have any clothes on, but I went to the door and he asked me to step out so he could show me something down the hall. When I stepped out just a bit, the door closed and it automatically locked by itself. "Hey! Look here," he said, as the rest of the crew ran and left me in the hall with no clothes and no key. Now you know that wasn't right, but that's the kind of things some railroad crews do to one another. They left to go to the bar, because they already got their sleep on the train. I got back in my room after an embarrassing episode. From then on, I never went out of the room without the key -- or clothes.

The next day we received our call. We got to the railroad engine and I sat down in the fireman's seat. Again, he asked me what I was doing over there. He was going to get his rest going home and I was running the train once more. I ran the train up The Slide and under the Omni, starting for Augusta. There's a lot of towns up along there, like Madison and Social Circle. When you go through the towns, you're not supposed to go more than 20 or 30 mph with the freight train. I went through this town, which I didn't know was there, after I came around this curve and, bam, there it was. When the crossing lights came on and the gate guards started coming down, the engine had already passed the crossing. I was going too fast because I didn't know where I was.

We came out of the town and went around the side of this mountain. Suddenly, I was on a curve going down hill. My feet were on the windshield of the train. That's how steep this hill was. I was looking straight down, using every brake I had. I looked back on the train and under every wheel was about a yard of fire shooting out from under them. It was really pretty. The scary conductor woke up among the commotion and ran over to see me leaning back in my chair with my feet on the window looking down the track with a trestle at the bottom.

This trestle was about 100 feet off the water. There was nothing but cross ties with two iron tracks running on the trestle and there I was flying too fast. You're only supposed to go 15 mph on the trestle. The engineer asked what was I going to do.

"There's nothing I can do until this big boy slows down," I said.

If you're going over the speed limit on a 15 mph trestle, you're probably going to derail. I could see that whole train dropping 100 feet to the little creek in the bottom. About that time that train went "whoa!" and when that engine got to that trestle it was probably going about 15 mph. I looked back and there wasn't any more fire coming out from under the wheels. I knocked off that engine brake and come out on it to get to pulling, because when you're going up the other side, you need to maintin that 15 mph to get over the hill. If you get too slow, your train is stuck on that trestle over the valley and you're going to have to wait until someone brings more engines to hook on and pull you over the hill. I knocked out the brake and came out on the engine throttle. There are eight positions on the throttle and I had that thing in eight by the time I got to the top, trying to pull that train over the hill. I got to the top, coming around 15 mph, then started going downhill. The engineer told me that was amazing and I was driving like one of the best engineers he'd seen. Then he asked how I did it, but I couldn't explain it. I don't know how I kept from killing everybody.

We got back and I worked the Athens switcher for a while after that. Then they told me I could go to Manchester, Georgia. Machester put me sort of back home near Columbus. I had five acres on Highway 27 just north of Columbus that I had bought a few years prior. I wanted to build a house there once, but I was working in Waycross.

In Manchester, I was running trains to Atlanta and back. I was also running trains to Birmingham, Alabama from Manchester. I made a few trips to Birmingham and they put me on the Talladega switcher. I ran that switcher for about three or four weeks. I no more got settled down good on that part of the track, when they called me in one night around 3 a.m. after working 12 hours and was told the clerk wanted to talk to me. The clerk said I would be reporting to Fitzgerald, Georgia. I said I wasn't going to say a word right now, because I don't trust myself to say something that will get me fired. So I went home, got my rest and got the official call to move to Fitzgerald. I didn't know it at the time, but Fitzgerald was the best place to work in the world. You'd run from Fitzgerald up to Manchester and back and then Fitzgerald to Waycross and back. It was a short line both ways and it was flat. No more straight up and straight down.

When I was running from Manchester to Birmingham I got to go across the Chattahoochee River and I got to run through tunnels going up to Birmingham. I thought that was really neat. The Nankipooh Flash had done got himself running through tunnels and across rivers.

Freedom on the rails.

CHAPTER 10 -- AFTER MANY YEARS, RECOGNITION

I was blessed to be inducted as a retired master sergeant into the Ranger Hall of Fame, at age 74, before a crowd at Ft. Benning in 2013. It was humbling to see my picture there among so many greats. I was one of 16 inductees in the 2013 Hall of Fame class, which included an Army chief of staff and three-star generals. That's pretty high cotton. Rangers are already an elite group, since so many soldiers who try do not make the cut. To be in that crowd is completely amazing. A few months earlier, I was inducted as a Distinguished Member of the Ranger Training Brigade at a ceremony also at Ft. Benning. My old Ranger buddy Max Haney, whom I saved from falling off a cliff during training, shared that story during my induction.

About a year later, I was invited to speak before about 200 distinguished people, about a third were active duty, about several Ranger honorees.

When people started gathering, the colonel told me he had a binder with his notes he was going to read. He showed me where he would introduce me and said I could place my notes in it so I'd have them at the lectern for what I assume was expected to be a lengthy speech. I told him I didn't need any notes. When I came up to speak, I grabbed the microphone out of its holder and started walking. I thanked the colonel and sergeant major for having me there and sponsoring the event to recognize superior Ranger instructors. My speech went like this:

The first thing I'd like to do is thank the wives, mothers, fathers and children of these men that stuck by them all these years of dedication. The unknown is harder than the known, so I'd much rather been over there getting shot up and the next day back eating steak or on stand down and knowing what's going on rather than the people back here not knowing day-to-day what's happening. So to these people, I give great thanks and appreciation for standing by these men, for there is no reason to go if unies have nothing to come back to. The saddest thing you will see is when a soldier is walking away from mail call with his head down when he doesn't get a letter from back home.

Now I want to talk about these inductees and honorees. The first one is Sgt. Armstrong. He had a small team of 10 men a mile and a half to two miles in front of American troops when they left Kuwait going to Baghdad. The Iraqi Army was between them and the American Army. They were really and truly the eye and ears of the Army, reporting everything that was happening behind Iraqi lines.

I'd also like to talk about Sgt. Bremen. He and his Ranger buddy were sponsored on Ready Rangers, which was a national weekly broadcast radio show reporting on the readiness and condition of the American army. They followed Ranger Bremen and his Ranger buddy Ricketts through Ranger school, reporting every week to the nation what they were going through back in 1951 when Ranger school was across Highway 27 and later it moved to the other side of Victory Drive beyond Todd Field where 44th Ranger Company and 3rd Ranger Company, where Sgt. Bremen was an instructor there.

I'd also like to thank Col. Guy, who is a middle school teacher now and he's retired. He was here in 44th Company and 3rd Ranger Company and also in patrolling committee and he briefed Walter Mondale when he was vice president and came to Ft. Benning and also Sgt. Perdue who demon-

strated for President Gerald Ford when he came to Benning. Sgt. Willie Block, Davey Lockett and I demonstrated for John F. Kennedy in October of 1961. Proverbs 22:29 says, "Watch a man who excels at his work and he will stand before kings." That's a very true statement.

These men have been selected to be honored to go down in history as some of the best Ranger instructors ever. They weren't satisfied to be soldiers, or paratroopers or even Airborne Rangers. They had to be Ranger instructors and now they're being recognized. But they have a terrible problem. They are addicted.

Back in my hometown, we have a fellow who has an addiction for scratch-offs. He cannot pass a 7-11 store without stopping and getting a handful of scratch-offs, whereas he lost his wife and his home. These men before you, their addiction is accomplishing the assigned mission. It's in every fiber of their body, mind, heart and soul. You tell them to do something and give them a mission and they will accomplish that mission.

Now I'd like to say a prayer. You don't have to close your eyes. You don't have to bow your heads. Our father, which art in heaven. Hallowed by thy name. Thy kingdom come. Thy will be done, on earth as it is in heaven. Give us this day our daily bread as we forgive those who trespass against us. Lead us not into temptation, but deliver us from evil, for thine is the kingdom and the power and the glory, forever and ever. Amen. Rangers lead the way.

I sat down amid a standing ovation. It can be risky for anybody to recite something like the Lord's Prayer before a crowd, because if you mess up everybody knows you messed up. And they don't forget that either.

They went on with the ceremony recognized the honorees. I still have people who were even there calling me and saying they heard I'd blowed them out this time and that the colonel said those were the best opening comments. A lot of guys get up there and they talk

30-45 minutes and people just want to leave. I spoke for seven minutes.

That's all the time I needed to accomplish my mission that day.

I had ultimately taken a payoff from CSX and retired again. My greatest accomplishment, however, was teaching Sunday school, working with youth groups and speaking about what God has done in my life at retreats and civic clubs, which I still do.

About the Author

It's a long way from rural Georgia to the jungles of Vietnam, but a journey shared by many young men from rural areas, small towns and big cities across the United States in the turbulent 1960s. It's even further from Vietnam to the Ranger Hall of Fame, but Thomas A. Bragg, Sr., made that journey, and shares it in the pages of this book.

As a youth, dyslexia stymied his formal education but did nothing to blunt is extraordinary native intelligence, his will to excel and his ultimate success. Being forced to leave home as a mere lad because there were too many other mouths to feed would have broken lesser men. But the severely malnourished seventeen-year-old who showed up at an Army recruiting office in Columbus, Georgia went on to a successful military career that would lead to his induction into the Ranger Hall of Fame.

Today, Thomas draws on his rich life experiences and deep faith to serve as a leader of his community and church. He lives with his wife Marji in his native Georgia.

Sgt. Bragg standing in front of E Co. LRRPS, 1st Platoon Headquarters in Tuy Hoa in 1967.

A Special Thanks

I would like to thank all of those who served with me in E Co. 20th Inf. (ABN) LRPs and C and G Company, 75th Ranger Regiment.

General Charles Getz, *a great commander*

Max Haney, *a great Ranger buddy*

Phil Mayer, *a great leader*

George Martin Arwood, *Streamered in*

Rick Ogden, (WIA)

Del Ayers, (WIA)

*Gary O'Neal

*Gary Dolan

*^Bill Block

*^Bob Gilbert

*^Milton (Davy) Lockett

Frederick William Weidner, (KIA)

Patrick Lee Henshaw, (KIA)

Sgt. Verlee, (WIA)

PFC Dobroski, (KIA)

~Don Thomason, *was in the battle of Tuy Hoa*

~Mike Burgas, Sgt Maj

~Gary Dalton, Sgt. Maj

~John Eden, L.T.

~Milton Hendrickson

~William Johnson

~Mike Kemble, (Doc)

~Everett Chess, Big House

~Randy Hayes

~Tim Mattingly

~Richard Spratley

~Dave Bechtold

~Don Chambers

~Brian Yost, *Cool man*

~Preston McGhee

~Mark Miller

~Darryl Benton

~Ray Bohrer, Sgt Maj

* Ranger Hall of Fame
^ Distinguished Member of the Ranger Training Brigade
~ LRP -- real men

RANGER CREED

Recognizing that I volunteered as a Ranger, fully knowing the hazards of my chosen profession, I will always endeavor to uphold the prestige, honor, and high esprit de corps of the Rangers.

Acknowledging the fact that a Ranger is a more elite Soldier who arrives at the cutting edge of battle by land, sea, or air, I accept the fact that as a Ranger my country expects me to move further, faster and fight harder than any other Soldier.

Never shall I fail my comrades. I will always keep myself mentally alert, physically strong and morally straight and I will shoulder more than my share of the task whatever it may be, one-hundred-percent and then some.

Gallantly will I show the world that I am a specially selected and well-trained Soldier. My courtesy to superior officers, neatness of dress and care of equipment shall set the example for others to follow.

Energetically will I meet the enemies of my country. I shall defeat them on the field of battle for I am better trained and will fight with all my might. Surrender is not a Ranger word. I will never leave a fallen comrade to fall into the hands of the enemy and under no circumstances will I ever embarrass my country.

Readily will I display the intestinal fortitude required to fight on to the Ranger objective and complete the mission though I be the lone survivor.

STANDING ORDERS, ROGERS' RANGERS
Major Robert Rogers, 1759

1. Don't forget nothing.

2. Have your musket clean as a whistle, hatchet scoured, sixty rounds powder and ball, and be ready to march at a minute's warning.

3. When you are on the march, act the way you would if you were sneaking up on a deer. See the enemy first.

4. Tell the truth about what you see and what you do. There is an army depending on us for correct information. You can lie all you please when you tell other folks about the rangers, but don't never lie to a ranger or officer.

5. Don't never take a chance you don't have to.

6. When we're on march we march single file, far enough apart so no one shot can go through two men.

7. If we strike swamps, or soft ground, we spread out abreast, so it's hard to track us.

8. When we march, we keep moving till dark, so as to give the enemy the least possible chance at us.

9. When we camp, half the party stays awake while the other half sleeps.

10. If we take prisoners, we keep 'em separate till we have time to examine them, so they can't cook up a story between 'em.

11. Don't ever march home the same way. Take a different route so you won't be ambushed.

12. No matter whether we travel in big parties or little ones, each party has to keep a scout 20 yards ahead, 20 yards on each flank, and 20 yards in the rear, so the main body can't be surprised and wiped out.

13. Every night you'll be told where to meet if surrounded by a superior force.

14. Don't sit down to eat without posting sentries.

15. Don't sleep beyond dawn. Dawn's when the French and Indians attack.

16. Don't cross a river at a regular ford.

17. If somebody's trailing you, make a circle, come back onto your own tracks, and ambush the folks that aim to ambush you.

18. Don't stand up when the enemy's coming against you. Kneel down, lie down, hide behind a tree.

19. Let the enemy come till he's almost close enough to touch. Then let him have it and jump out and finish him up with your hatchet.

Made in the USA
Charleston, SC
18 October 2015